Fathers of the Covenant

*Some Great Chapters
in Genesis and Exodus*

FATHERS OF THE COVENANT

STUDIES IN GENESIS AND EXODUS

H.L.Ellison

Ronald N. Haynes Publishers, Inc.
PALM SPRINGS CALIFORNIA

FATHERS OF THE COVENANT

Ronald N. Haynes Publishers, Inc.
Palm Springs, California 92263

First USA Edition 1981

LIBRARY OF CONGRESS CATALOG CARD NUMBER: 81-83171
ISBN 0-88021-019-2 (previously 0-85364-220-6)

Printed in the United States of America

Originally published by
THE PATERNOSTER PRESS
PATERNOSTER HOUSE
3 MOUNT RADFORD CRESENT
EXETER UK EX2 4JW
ENGLAND

TO
MY WIFE
who for forty years has been
lover, companion and partner
by the grace of God.

Contents

Abbreviations

In addition to standard literary abbreviations, the usual ones for the names of the books of the Bible are used. In addition the following may need special mention.

AV	Authorized or King James's Version (1611)
HDB	Hastings's Dictionary of the Bible – 5 vol. edn.
JB	The Jerusalem Bible (1966)
JPS	OT issued by Jewish Publication Society (1917)
Knox	Ronald Knox, *The Holy Bible* (1945, 1949)
LXX	Septuagint – the standard Greek translation of OT made between 200 and 50 B.C.
mg.	margin
Moffatt	J. Moffatt, *A New Translation of the Bible* (1913, 1926)
NBD	The New Bible Dictionary (1962)
NEB	The New English Bible (1961, 1970)
RSV	Revised Standard Version (1946, 1952)
RV	Revised Version (1881, 1885)
Skinner	Genesis (The International Critical Commentary)
Speiser	Genesis (The Anchor Bible)

(*Abbreviations continued*)

von Rad	Genesis (Old Testament Library)
TEV	Today's English Version – Good News Bible (1966, 1976)
tx.	text

Where two dates are given, the former is that of the NT, the latter of the OT.

PREFACE

My teaching of the Old Testament has over the years of
necessity involved me in technical questions of various
kinds. However interesting these may at times have been,
my main interest and pleasure have always lain in its exposition, i.e. the discovery, not simply of its linguistic meaning, but above all of its spiritual message, with its timeless
revelation of God's will and character.

The writing of these studies, eleven of which first
appeared in *The Hebrew Christian*, the quarterly organ of the
Hebrew Christian Alliance, has been a labour of love, and it
has given me great pleasure that they have been considered
worth a more permanent form and a wider circle of readers.

The exposition has been based on RSV, but all the more
widely used translations have been referred to. The frequent
references to traditional Jewish interpretation can be
explained by the interests of the original readers, but they
should be of value to a wider circle, both when they are
correct and also when they have little validity.

Numerous Hebrew words have been given in transliteration, so that those interested can carry out some linguistic
research on their own, even if they know no Hebrew. The
transliteration used is the simplified one employed by
Young's Analytical Concordance, except that *h* is used in
preference to the gutteral *ch*, and that the two gutterals,
normally unpronounced in modern Hebrew, Aleph and

Ayin are represented by ' and '; *q* has the sound of *k* pronounced far back in the mouth.

My hope and prayer are that these chapters may cause their readers to study the Old Testament more deeply for themselves, for it was of the Old Testament that Paul wrote, "All scripture is inspired by God and profitable".

CHAPTER 1

CREATION
(*Gen. 1:1–2:3*)

We are all apt to take words at their face value and to blame those who do not live up to what they say as liars or hypocrites. It is true that few are as frank as a sharp-tongued college friend of mine, who told me one day, "You must not take what I say too seriously, for my words serve as a mask to hide my real feelings," but there are many like him.

My experience is that when I meet someone who has a lot to say about faith, I can generally sense an underlying feeling of tension and anxiety, a desire to be confirmed in what he so ardently affirms. Normally true faith is so much part of the one who possesses it, that he largely takes it for granted and is little inclined to speak of it. It is easy to understand that the one who speaks much of faith is often looking out for things that can strengthen and confirm it. If he is an Evangelical Christian he seeks especially anything that will confirm the truth and inspiration of the Bible, such as the discoveries of archaeology, though these are seldom as unambiguous as is hoped.

To such seekers I have repeatedly commended the opening chapter of the Bible. It possesses a quality which is almost certainly unique. When we compare it with the efforts of pre-scientific man to explain the existence of the world and all in it, or with those of the modern scientist trying to make clear to the scientifically unversed, or even to those of his colleagues, who are involved in other disci-

plines, how life came into being, there is a certain luminosity and self-evidence about the Genesis account that are
not shared by any of its rivals.

That is not all. The child and the illiterate can hear the
biblical account read and gain a self-consistent and intelligible picture, while the man of science, weary after a day's
work in the laboratory, can relax as he reads the story and
acknowledge that here is a more convincing and satisfying
picture than his detailed studies can offer.

We may go further. As the history of Bible translation
shows, this story of creation can be rendered intelligibly
into almost all the languages of mankind. There are those
living in the frozen wastes of the Arctic for whom some of
its concepts cannot be adequately expressed, and the same
may be true of some whose home is in deserts far from the
sea, or other great sheets of water, but these form a minute
fraction of the earth's population.

Some profess disappointment, when they compare its
language with the pronouncements of modern science. Had
its language reflected the knowledge and concepts of the
time of Moses, or indeed of any other Old Testament
writer, it would long ago have been outdated. Had it
embodied the knowledge and language of the second half of
the twentieth century, it would have remained a closed
chapter until our time, only to become outdated for our
children. As it is, however, for at least eight hundred generations, it has brought to men the essential spiritual facts
behind God's creating.

From it we know that nothing has come into being apart
from God or exists in its own right, as is claimed by Materialism. Similarly there is no suggestion of Pantheism,
which in various forms has been so popular in the past and
still is today. It does not allow that nature is in any sense
divine, or a sort of extension of God. Equally it excludes the
idea that God is in some way part of nature and so ultimately
subject to its laws.

While it has nothing to tell us of how God's will, expressed by his word, went into operation, it makes quite clear that it knows nothing of the common, modern evolutionary theory, by which mindless and impersonal nature, working according to laws, of which it is ignorant, has learnt to create the universe, as we know it today. In place of this we have divine intelligence, working out its purposes towards a predetermined goal, and ending with the verdict of "very good", i.e. exactly as willed and planned.

Not only did God place the imprint of his power and wisdom on all that he had made, cf. Rom. 1:20 – something to which the discoveries of the natural sciences continually bear witness, though those that make them not seldom do their best to explain the facts away – but he stamped mankind, both man and woman (v. 27), the summit and climax of creation, with his image and likeness.

The theological implications of this expression will not be developed here – the whole of Scripture is in one sense a commentary on it – but it clearly implies two things. First of all man was made capable of knowing God and entering into a living relationship with him, and secondly it made it possible, when the time was ripe, for God to become man.

In our days the story has for many largely lost its force, because it has become the theme of polemic discussions alien to its nature and purpose. Because it has so often been forgotten that its purpose is to reveal God and not scientific knowledge, ever since the rise of modern science, many have tried to force their understanding of it on science and its discoveries. In order to maintain their own integrity many scientists have mistakenly felt it necessary to depreciate Genesis 1.

An outstanding example is the controversy about the meaning of "day", which occurs thirteen times in this section. Though in 2:4 twenty-four hours cannot be its meaning, for many it became a test of orthodoxy, and for some it still is, that it must be understood as twenty-four hours in 1:5, 8, etc., in spite of the apparently conclusive evidence offered by the natural sciences, that it must be understood as a long period of time. In addition it seems clear from the absence of the concluding formula, "And there was evening and there was morning . . ." for the seventh day, when God kept *shabat*, desisted from his work of creation[1], that this day has never ended, the work of creation having been completed for good and all.

The worthy, but inadequate, motivation for this seems to be mainly that they think that God's glory is enhanced by postulating creation over a short period rather than over long ages. Once we are prepared to accept God's power and wisdom, there seems to be no reason for preferring the instantaneous, which so appeals to short-lived man, to a purpose working itself out over long ages.

In fact, the whole controversy may well be an example of much ado about nothing. There seem to be only two serious suggestions about the origin of Genesis 1. It can be held, with many Old Testament scholars, that during the Babylonian exile, Judean priests came to know the Babylonian cosmological myths, as enshrined in the *enuma elish*, and eliminated all the crude mythological and polytheistic elements, and so produced the Biblical account. It is, of course, possible to believe that the Spirit of God should so have guided them, but for me it is far easier to accept that it was direct revelation from the first. If it was revelation, it is far more likely to have been partially in vision than purely in words; in other words the whole process of creation passed before the prophet's inner eye in six instalments. If that is so, though the days would still coincide with major divisions in the history of creation, they would refer primarily to the recipient of the revelation.[2]

---

[1] The usual rendering "rested" comes from a misunderstanding of the Hebrew, which means to stop doing a thing, desisting from it, which normally for us implies having a rest.

[2] The concept of days of revelation was popularized in England by P. J. Wiseman, *Creation Revealed in Six Days* (1949),* but he had been anticipated by J. H. Kurtz in Germany about a century earlier. (*See facing page.*)

Similarly, there have been many and still are some, who wishing to avoid the apparent evidence of fossil remains, have translated v. 2, "The earth became without form and void", and have sought confirmation in Isa. 46:18. A little more attention to Hebrew grammar would have saved them from this;[1] they might then have realized that what to man might seem formless chaos, for God could be the building blocks for an ordered universe.

Some of the objections raised by modern science tend to be based on traditional renderings, e.g. the firmament of v. 6 (*raqia'*), which could equally well be translated expanse, cf. Isa. 40:22, and the use of water, where the relatively modern term gas is clearly implied.

Most of the scientific scorn today is reserved for the work of the fourth day. It is claimed that Genesis teaches that sun, moon and stars were not created until relatively late in the process of creation. We can forget the stars, for there is fairly general agreement that this is a parenthetic remark. But what of the sun and moon? The weakest element in very much Old Testament scholarship since the middle of last century has been its consistent underestimate of the intelligence of its writers. It offers no evidence that any thought that the earth's light came otherwise than from the sun, and in lesser extent from the moon.

Without taking refuge in the suggestion, which may well be correct, but is unprovable, that until the fourth day clouds and vapour cut off any direct sight of sun and moon, it is sufficient to point out that in vv. 14–19 the main stress is not on the creation of sun and moon but on their function. It could well be that this is mentioned here in parallelism to the work of the first day, but it is more likely to be in anticipation of the work of the fifth day. The story does not define life, but reserves the term "living creature" (*nephesh ḥayyah*) to those beings that have the power of independent

---

[1] The rendering suggested demands a change of *Hayetah* to *wa-tehi*.

* Revised edition in *Clues to Creation in Genesis*, London, 1977.

motion. They all, in varying degree and manner are subject
to the great rhythms of day and night and of the seasons,
which are marked by sun and moon.

The end of God's creating had prepared the stage for
man's work. As the next chapter will show, the "very
good" of 1:31 does not imply that there was nothing for him
to do. Good (*tob*) in Hebrew does not carry with it the same
degree of moral or physical perfection that it may have in
English, and here it need mean no more than that creation,
at the end of God's activity, was exactly as he had planned
it. "He found it very pleasing" (Speiser). "Subdue" and
"have dominion over" (literally, tread down) in 1:28 are
strong expressions, which imply that man would have a
major task and high honour, as he faced strong opposition
in enforcing the perfect rule of the God he was representing
throughout the world.

Additional Note
Genesis 1:1f

In contrast to the simple and majestic opening words, "in
the beginning God created the heavens and the earth", with
which the account of creation begins, RSV, NEB, TEV, in
text or in margin, but not JB, prefer to render, "In the
beginning of creation, when God made heaven and earth,
the earth was without form and void . . ." This is supported
by a number of modern commentators, e.g. Skinner,
Speiser, but not von Rad.

This rendering is not new, for it was suggested in somewhat varying forms by Rashi and Ibn Ezra, two of the
greatest of the mediaeval Jewish commentators, and it is
entirely compatible with Hebrew syntax. Its present popu-
larity is in part due to a desire to avoid the suggestion that
God created chaos, a difficulty, which we have seen, has
troubled some of very different views.

It seems difficult, however, to believe that in a chapter of
majestic simplicity, which was almost certainly intended

for public recitation, the author would have begun with such a highly complicated sentence. Apart from the two rabbis named, the traditional rendering is universal in rabbinic exegesis, and it is found in all the earlier translations. In addition there can be little doubt that Jn.1:1 is a deliberate reference to it.

Those wishing for a comprehensive discussion will find it in W. Eichrodt, *In the Beginning*, in *Israel's Prophetic Heritage*, edited by B. W. Anderson and W. Harelson (SCM, 1962).

In addition NEB renders, "and a mighty wind swept over the surface of the waters", which is reflected in TEV mg. This is supported by von Rad, with an unconvincing reference to Dan. 7:2, and Speiser, "an awesome wind". It is perfectly true that Elohim (God) is occasionally used to express a superlative, but this is rare, and normally poetic. It seems intrinsically improbable that in a chapter where Elohim appears thirty-two times, and another three times in 2:1–3, that it should have to be taken metaphorically in this one instance. Here again, all tradition speaks against the modern understanding.

CHAPTER 2

MAN'S NATURE AND FALL
(Gen. 2, 3)

Genesis 1 is above all concerned with God as Creator. This is followed by a revelation of man's nature and fall. That man is the centre of interest is shown by the name Jehovah[1] being attached to Elohim (2:4, and some twenty times in the two chapters). Elohim is the God of power, whose existence may be known from nature (Rom. 1:19, 20); Jehovah is the God of personal revelation. This almost unique usage here is probably to stress that Jehovah who deals with man is identical with the Creator of the universe. In these chapters Elohim by itself is used only in the conversation between the snake and Eve, thus showing how little either knew of the true nature of God.

Here we are concerned with man rather than with creation in general. It is this change of stance which causes the differences in the story of man's creation, which puzzle the simple and give scope to the theories of liberals and lovers of fancy. Here the story seems to go back in its essentials to Adam and to God's answer to his enquiry how he came to be. We have no right to create gratuitous difficulties by generalizing from statements applicable only to Adam himself.[2]

[1] I use Jehovah as the form most familiar to English readers of the Bible in preference to Yahweh, which is almost certainly the name under which Israel worshipped its covenant God. Its meaning is discussed in ch.9.

[2] In spite of the arguments in E. K. V. Pearce, *Who was Adam?*, I cannot accept that Gen.1 refers to paleolithic man, but Gen. 2 to neolithic man. I have no theory as to when the hominoids we know from the fossil record became man in the biblical sense.

Many and varied have been man's speculations about the cradle of the human race. The general impression created by Scripture and seemingly supported by archaeology is that it was somewhere in the Near East, and this is confirmed by the mention of the Tigris and Euphrates in 2:14. No certain identification of the other two rivers has been offered. Irrespective of our interpretation of the details of Noah's Flood, we must allow for major physical changes which may have been caused by it.

In the description of the creation of man (2:7) we find God forming (the verb is used of a potter at his work) *'adam* (man, i.e. mankind) from the dust of the tillable ground (*'adamah*); into his nostrils he breathed the breath (*neshamah*) of life, and so man becomes a living soul (*nephesh*), a living being.

The words used demand our closer attention. *'adam* stands in Hebrew for mankind in general and includes the female as well as the male. He is here an individual only because he is the beginning; Eve is part of him. Not until 4:25, when there are children, does it become a proper name. Adam, i.e. mankind, is linked by his body-stuff to all God's physical creation and especially to his fellow-men, from whom he cannot live in isolation (Rom. 14:7). There is no real word for a living body in the Old Testament. We, basing ourselves on Greek thought, look on our bodies as the definers of ourselves. All in my body is I, all outside is not I. In Hebrew, however, "flesh" stresses my essential oneness with others.

My true individuality is not created by my body, but by my spirit. If *neshamah* is used here instead of the more usual *ruah*, it is probably to guard against the idea, usual in pantheistic religions and sometimes present in some Christian circles, that man has a spark of the Divine in him. There seems otherwise to be little or no difference in the use of the two words.

These two, flesh and spirit, fuse into a single whole, the *nephesh*, which is usually but misleadingly rendered soul.

My "soul" is the whole of me, the essential man, who knows the physical world through his flesh and makes himself known through it, while through his spirit he is in touch with God and the spirit-world. That which we generally mean by soul is normally expressed in Hebrew by "heart".

The first man was created in arid steppe country (2:5) – the mention of its not having rained must surely be interpreted in this context – before being moved into the garden which God had prepared in Eden away to the east. The obvious inference is that Adam was so to carry out his work in the garden, that he and his family would gradually extend it until it had embraced the whole world. In the mean time he was to guard it; such is the basic and natural meaning of the verb rendered to keep it or care for it (2:15). The form that evil might take was not told him, but he was warned that danger existed.

Just as Adam had to experience the bleakness of nature before he was transferred to the glories of the garden, so too he had to face loneliness and incompleteness before his need was met. First, however, he had to begin his work of authority and dominion. God brought the animals and birds to him, partly because being wild they would not have come spontaneously, partly to make it clear to the man that his authority was a delegated one. To give a person the right to name man or beast implied both an understanding of his nature and also authority over him, cf. Gen. 41:45, 2 Ki. 23:34; 24:17, Dan. 1:7. The very exercise of his authority impressed his aloneness on Adam. Though the animals had been brought under his authority, Adam knew that their very subjection made it impossible for them to be true partners.

The story of the creation of woman (2:21, 22) has been interpreted in the most diverse ways, from the most literal to the most abstrusely scientific. Here let it be mentioned only that the word traditionally translated "rib" almost

certainly does not mean this – the various rabbinic suggestions bear testimony to this – but more probably "side".
What is important is that every human being is derived
ultimately not from two persons but from one; Eve is
female Adam. The virgin birth of Jesus, his humanity
derived from one person, marked Him out as a new creation, the last Adam.

The statement in 2:18 is general and applies to a woman
equally with a man (the word used is *'adam*); God meets the
man's need with more than a companion. He provides
someone who really suits him, a partner (NEB). This partnership, with its differentiation of sex and all that flows
from it, was implicit in God's creational purpose (1:27), and
was not an afterthought. The only reason for the delay in
his creating of Eve was to make Adam realize his need for
her. They were not to be drawn together by mere sexual
instinct and urge. Celibacy, where it is not the direct result
of human sin and violence (Matt. 19:12), or of a malfunc-
tioning of the body, directly or indirectly the outcome of
sin, may come from the hermit's life or from a refusal of
marriage. In either case the person embracing the single life
risks damaging his personality or worse, unless he is called
to a single life by God, who can give him or her abundant
grace for the purpose.

The married state equally calls for the enabling grace of
God. The cultural background both of the Bible and of
modern life assumes that the bride will leave her home, her
clan, her people it may be. In becoming one with her
husband she is caught up into his world and family. But
such is not God's purpose; "A man leaves his father and his
mother and cleaves to his wife, and they become one flesh"
(2:24). "Flesh" is used presumably because in their unity
each retains his personal responsibility to God. This statement means that, without in any way denying the principle
of the fifth commandment, under God the husband belongs
in the first place to his wife, even as she does to him. They
cannot become one, if either is still tied in part to the past.

This should make it abundantly clear, that whatever may be said in the Bible, especially in the New Testament, about the subordination of the wife to her husband may not be interpreted in any way as meaning that she is his inferior in any sense, or that he has the right to dominate her life.

In the garden two fruit trees are singled out for mention, the tree of the knowledge of good and evil and the tree of life. There is no room for magic in God's creation. There is nothing created that can give life purely because it is eaten, and similarly nothing that can impart knowledge in the same way. The powers of the two trees lay not in their nature but in the role that God had imparted to them. There is no suggestion that an animal feeding on them would have acquired either wisdom or length of life.

The usual assumption is that Adam and Eve were in the position of young children, completely unaware that anything was right or wrong, and that the eating of the fruit imparted that knowledge. There are two fatal objections to this view. A being completely ignorant of moral right and wrong could hardly be said to have been created in the image and likeness of God. In addition, had they not known that it was right and good to obey God, wrong and evil to disobey him, we could hardly call their disobedience sin. However we define sin, we infer previous knowledge. If we think of it as missing the mark, we imply knowledge of a mark to be hit. If we think of it as lawlessness (1 Jn. 3:4), we imply the recognition of a binding law.

We shall find the probable answer in a peculiarity of the human child. To a greater or less degree, but never perfectly in more developed life, a young animal knows what is good and what is bad for it. This instinctive knowledge exists even when the young one has been taken from its dam at the earliest possible moment. This instinctive knowledge, however, is conspicuously lacking in the human child and, for that matter, adult also. Even so we must assume that Adam and Eve had to depend on God to know what the physical outcome of their actions would be. That such is the meaning of the knowledge of good and evil is supported by 2 Sam. 14:17, Isa. 7:15, as well as by its use among the men of Qumran.

The story of the temptation is simple and straight-forward; some light is thrown on what lies behind it by later Scripture, but we are intended to understand it as it is, even though some elements are probably symbolic. We need not ask ourselves how man and animals could communicate. The ability is implicit in man's position of lordship. Equally we are not to concern ourselves how the snake was influenced by Satan. What we must reject is the idea that Satan disguised himself as a snake or borrowed the snake's body for the occasion.

It is likely that the snake in its cleverness resented man's domination and was therefore open to Satan's suggestions. In apparent simplicity it asked, "Surely God did not say, 'You shall not eat of *any* tree of the garden'?" As is so often the case, the attack was not through what was but through what could be. By speaking purely of God the snake implied that since it knew God only as the All-Powerful, such behaviour by him would be quite possible.

By using "God" in her answer, Eve, instead of teaching the snake her higher knowledge of God, came down to its level. She soon betrayed part of the reason. To the prohib-ition of eating she added that of touching, but where did she get this idea? One feature of God's revelation is that he very rarely, if ever, repeated his commands, where their pur-pose was clear. Having warned Adam (2:16, 17), there was no reason why he should repeat it to Eve; that was her husband's task. We can hardly avoid the conclusion that he was playing for safety by adding "nor touch it"; this is another way of saying that he did not fully trust God, when he gave him Eve, and this doubt will soon have communi-cated itself to her.

Once the snake realized that Eve shared its doubts, there came the charge that God was trying to keep man in thrall by withholding the knowledge that would set him free. He could become like God, not in creatorial power but in freedom, dependent on none. Even though AV "gods" has LXX backing, there is little to be said for it.

There seems to be little gained by linking 1 Jn. 2:16 with the stages of Eve's downfall (3:6). Eyes and heart in rebellion against God will always see things in a false light. There is no suggestion that there was anything about this tree and its fruit to mark it out. We may emphatically reject the rabbinic conceit that the snake pushed Eve against the tree, thus showing her that she had not died, even though she had touched it. It was an outcome of the rabbinic minimizing of the reality of sin and of the Fall. Even less acceptable is the rabbis' suggestion that the snake wanted Adam out of the way so as to have Eve for itself.

We are assured by Paul that "Adam was not deceived, but the woman was deceived and became a transgressor" (1 Tim. 2:14). So we should ask ourselves why he, too, ate of the fruit. The only satisfactory answer seems to be that he decided he would stand by his wife, come what might. It was an admirable sentiment, but betrayed complete lack of trust in the possibility of divine forgiveness and restoration. If we must draw up a scale of guilt, it should be clear that Adam's was indubitably greater than his wife's. Doubt of God's love seems to have started with him, and it led to his deliberate defiance of God's will.

The first obvious result of their disobedience was their realization that they were naked. There is nothing in the story to justify the idea, still sometimes met, that until then they had been enveloped in radiance, which served as a garment, and that this had suddenly disappeared. Rather, this is the supreme anticlimax. It all happened as the snake had promised (v. 4); their eyes were opened, and they saw that they were naked ...! But we should go further than this. There is much in the Bible conveyed by allusion, virtually symbolically, and this is the case here. It implies that there was an immediate deterioration in the relationship between them, a breach in their oneness.

The reason is easy to find. Unity in the demonic and animal world implies domination or even absorption.[1] For two independent and equal personalities to co-exist in harmony they must move around a common centre, which is, of course, God. With the removal of that centre the harmony between husband and wife was marred, for each wished to be the centre around which the other should move. Human sin almost always hits the marriage partner first and the children next.

Worse was to come. There are mysteries about the conscience that the psychologist has never plumbed. Their nakedness, which had troubled their relationship and which they had tried to hide, was now suddenly seen as involving their relationship to God also (3:8–10), and the fig-leaf covering did not avail with him. Adam's noble desire to stand by his wife evaporated once sin began to separate them, and selfishness took over. Without hesitation he placed the whole blame on Eve, and even on God himself, for he had given him the woman (3:12). Eve's laying of the blame on the snake (3:13) had more justification, but there was no confession of her share in what had happened.

It is essential to notice that in God's sentence a curse is pronounced on the physical creation but not on Adam and Eve, who were merely reaping what they had sowed. Pedersen[2] is probably correct in saying that the relationship between sin and curse is as that between righteousness and blessing. In other words, even as sin separates from God so it separates from his blessing.

It is a matter of controversy whether we should render "Because you have done this you are accursed more than all cattle and wild creatures" (NEB), or "Cursed art thou from

---

[1] Cf. Screwtape's words to Wormwood, "We want cattle who can finally become food; He wants servants who can finally become sons. We want to suck in, He wants to give out. We are empty and would be filled; He is full and flows over." (C. S. Lewis, *The Screwtape Letters*, p. 47.)

[2] Pedersen, *Israel* I–II, p. 437.

among all cattle . . ." (JPS). If one takes curse in the sense
given above and remembers a passage like Rom. 8:19–22,
the former rendering becomes the more probable. It was
God's will that the fullness of his blessing should come to
nature through mankind. With the fall of man that blessing
was cut off. The snake's posture had been its glory, cf.
Prov. 30:19, but now it was to be the outward sign of its
humiliation and defeat.

It is very generally stated that the curse contains an old
explanation why men are instinctively hostile to the snake.
Such an explanation does not tell us why the enmity should
be particularly with the woman. God was looking beyond
what had happened to what lay behind it. The promise was
addressed to the snake rather than to Eve, for it was primarily an expression of the sovereignty of God, rather than an
expression of God's mercy, cf. Ezek. 36:22. It spoke of a
long struggle between man and the powers that would seek
to destroy him, and of ultimate triumph after suffering. The
stress on the woman and her seed could be understood only
long after, when the fulfilment came.

It should be noted that the curse did not exclude from
God's care. The snake had its allotted place in the Ark, and
we find it on the transformed earth no longer a source of
death and disgust (Isa. 11:8), even though the far distant past
would not be forgotten (Isa. 65:25).

As for Adam and Eve, they would be touched in that
where they could glory most. The woman's supreme glory
is that from her comes new life, and in the giving of life she
would be reminded of what she once did. More than that:
whatever her motive she deliberately drew her husband
after her into disobedience, so "your desire (*teshuqah*) will
be for your husband". The word *teshuqah* is found only
twice more; in Gen. 4:7 it is used of the wild beast's longing
for its prey, and in Cant. 7:10, where passionate desire is
probably meant. The woman's love was to degenerate into
the expression of deep-rooted passions, and the result
would be "He will rule over you". It is regrettable that

virtually all translations render "he shall rule over you"; TEV is a welcome exception. There is no command here but a plain statement of fact, that man in his selfishness would take advantage of his wife's weakness to enforce his will on her, instead of treating her as his equal and partner.

It can hardly be overstressed that in Eph. 5:23–33, where the wife's subjection to her husband in everything is stressed, it is linked with the command, "Husbands, love your wives, as Christ loved the church and gave himself up for her." Where husbands do not obey this command, they can hardly expect their wives' "subjection in everything". It is an evil thing to appeal to Scripture, when it suits our purpose, and to forget or ignore those statements that make unwelcome claims upon us.

NEB, JB, TEV are correct in rendering "to the man" in 3:17; this is something that involves all mankind irrespective of sex. Mankind was to have dominion over nature, but now he was to find that even the soil revolted against him. Whether it is toil of hands or of brain, man always discovers that to whatever earthly Paradise he comes, whatever Shangri-la he finds, that ease destroys him and nature plays him false. Rabbinic exegesis, presumably to minimize the results of sin, insists on the basis of Gen. 5:29; 8:21 that the curse on the ground was only for Adam's lifetime, but human experience hardly bears this out. Perhaps if more of the rabbis had been agriculturists, they would have been less confident.

Man, made in the image and likeness of God, is to be earth-bound, returning at the last to the dust from which he had been taken. The warning had been that in the day they ate of the tree they would die. The Fall did not destroy the image in which they had been created, but it so marred it, that between man's spirit and God a barrier had been created. His spirit was lamed; it could no longer function as it should, and so man became less than man. Thus Paul could say of Jesus that he was the second man (1 Cor. 15:47). A careful study of death and dying in the Old Testament will

probably convince the student, that though in the vast
majority of cases little if any discernable difference can be
found between the Hebrew and the English concepts, yet
from time to time we find cases where the meaning of the
Hebrew seems to be above all that of impotence and non-
functioning. Indeed this is the basic concept behind existence in Sheol (the abode of the dead; in Greek, Hades). It
would seem that this, not unconsciousness or non-
existence, lies at the root of the Hebrew concept of death.

Since fallen man could no longer function for the purpose
for which he had been created, he had in fact died in the hour
of sinning, even though the return to dust lay yet many
years ahead. To drag out one's days without purpose is a
mockery and misery, and this is symbolized by the barring
of the way to the tree of life.

Just as God did not withdraw his protective care from the
world as a whole, cf. Gen. 6:19–21, Jonah 4:11, so he did not
from man either. The token of this was his making gar-
ments of skin for Adam and Eve. Many see in this the
institution of sacrifice, but we are hardly justified in deduc-
ing this from the silence of Scripture, the more so as the
story of Cain and Abel, rightly understood, does not suggest that the rejection of Cain's sacrifice was due to any
shortcomings in its form, i.e. no animal had had to lay
down its life, but rather to the fact of an unacceptable life
(4:7). We do not have the right to use the silences of Scripture to force what is said into the straitjackets of our dogma-
tic systems. Since sacrifice plays such an important role in
the Old Testament, one could reasonably expect that there
would be a plain statement, if this were really the Divine
institution of it.

Remarkably enough these chapters are not referred to,
except obliquely, in the rest of the Old Testament, and only
sparingly in the New. The reason is not far to seek. Man
rebels against the concept of the sins of the fathers being
visited upon their children to the third and fourth genera-

tion. He repeatedly dreams that he can mount higher on the ruins of the past, that he can "build Jerusalem in England's green and pleasant land".

Though history reveals again and again that each generation pays for the follies of previous ones, yet there are always those who think that by revolution or education they can so change things that the entail of the past will be broken. This optimism shows itself as clearly in religious circles as in secular walks of life. Even the theologians who most stress original sin and the depravity of man seem normally to forget their doctrines when they leave the study or pulpit.

Rather than harping continually on this fact in his revelation, God preferred, having given us the story of the original fall, to drive the lesson home by giving us the history of man in its failure, first in the world at large and then in his chosen people Israel. While Gen. 3 receives no direct mention in the Old Testament, almost every page is a commentary on it.

There is perhaps some excuse for the philosopher in the Greek tradition, with its stress on the spirit of man and depreciation of the material, when he rejects the concept of original sin. This excuse does not hold for the rabbi, the Marxist and the psychologist, who in one way or another stress the importance of the physical and of society as a whole. Indeed, the Christian doctrine is not that Jesus Christ sets a man free from his past so that he may exist in a vacuum until his final salvation comes, he sets him free so as to put him into a new society, the Church, the body of Christ, where every influence should be toward righteousness and the accomplishment of God's will and purpose, but even there we find the dark stains of failure throughout its history.

Man ate; and man acquired knowledge at phenomenal speed even in the antediluvian period. He has gone on, until today he seems to be on the verge of unlocking the ultimate secrets of nature. But what he has not acquired is the ability to understand the wisdom and purpose behind creation, the "why?" of things. Equally he has not learned how to use his knowledge for his and nature's good, or to be more fair, even when he has known, there has been a deep-rooted weakness of moral fibre, which has prevented him from applying his knowledge in practice.

Some who have read this chapter will have smiled with some feeling of superiority at its simplistic treatment of what they call a parable, or more likely, and misleadingly, a myth. So be it. Yet I doubt, whether, in spite of all their superior understanding of what happened at the dawn of man's history, they will be able to deduce other or deeper spiritual truths from it. There are times when God has to use the language of the nursery in teaching men the cause of their failure, and we shall lose nothing in accepting the lesson in the way it has been given us.

CHAPTER 3

ABRAM THE HEBREW
(*Gen. 12*)

As the centuries rolled by, the Flood and its message became an increasingly dim memory. Everywhere men turned once more to the worship of the forces of nature, even though the dim memory of a supreme creator God, lingered on. It was obscured by the apparent reality of the great forces of nature, which by their underlying harmony, yet frequent discord, suggested a family of gods who, while closing their ranks against evil spirits from outside, yet vied among themselves in jealous quarrels for their greater influence and honour.

In spite of wide local differences, it is permissible to generalize about the nature-religion of Bible lands. There was a fairly common cultural pattern in the East Mediterranean lands and Mesopotamia, and scholars are accustomed to speak of a common cultic pattern. It was generally believed that the great gods had produced order out of chaos. They had then created man for their own ends, that man might serve them, feed them by their sacrifices, and honour them in ways many and various, which would help the gods to hold any forces of chaos in check that might once again raise their heads.

Speaking generally, the demands of the gods tended to be ritual rather than moral, except in so far as morality would uphold the stability of society. They themselves were above morality, sometimes even immoral. Since they were the

great forces which controlled natural phenomena, they
were ultimately subject to nature as a whole. They had
shared out the earth and sea and the underworld among
themselves, and according to where a man found himself,
he was under obligation to give special, but not exclusive,
honour to the god of that area. Animistic concepts, which
used to figure so largely up to fifty years ago in books on
Genesis, had by the time of Abram, some 2000 B.C., been
superseded, leaving only vestiges in popular religion.

Joshua testified to the fact that Terah, a descendant of
Shem, shared in the idolatry around him, and that its memory had never completely died out among his descendants
(Jos. 24:2). From the few indications given us in Scripture it
seems clear that this idolatry was of the general West-
Semitic type, without the grosser sexual elements that had
so poisoned Canaanite religion.

No indication of any kind is given us how Abram came to
faith in one true God, and we know almost as little about the
intellectual content of that faith. We may dismiss without
discussion the rabbinic idea that he knew the essentials of
all that was to be revealed later, and that he perfectly kept
the Mosaic law, though many centuries were to pass before
it was given. Slightly less improbable are the traditional
stories of how Abram came to faith.[1] In fact they throw
more light on Jewish propaganda methods against idolatry
in the time of Christ than they do on Abram.

We are first introduced to Abram in two accounts which
seem to have an element of contradiction in them. In the
former (11:31, 32) we find Terah leaving Ur of the Chaldees
to go to Canaan but interrupting his journey in Haran,
where he died. No reasons are given for his leaving Ur, or
for his stopping in Haran. In the latter story the call of God
comes to Abram in a place unspecified, though at first sight
it would seem to be Haran, telling him to leave country,
relatives and "his father's house" for a land not named, but

---

[1] See additional Note at end of chapter.

which later turns out to be Canaan.

Superficially it might seem that consciously or unconsciously Terah initiated the divine purpose and after his death (Acts 7:4) Abram was commanded to continue it. There are, however, difficulties in accepting this view. The natural interpretation of the figures given is that Abram left Haran before his father's death, though this must not be pressed. There are considerable variations between the chronological figures given in the early versions, and those in the Samaritan leave Abram in Haran until his father died. More important is that in this case he could hardly have been commanded to leave his "father's house". Most important of all is that in 15:7 God tells him, "I am the Lord who brought you from Ur of the Chaldeans", a statement taken up in Neh. 9:7, Acts 7:3.

The most likely explanation is that we have here perhaps the first example of that dualism in story-telling which is not uncommon in the Bible, though perhaps we should regard the two creation stories as the first example. We have the story first as men saw it. Terah set out from Ur of the Chaldeans with most of his family. Whether Nahor moved to Paddan-Aram earlier or later (Gen. 22:20–24; 24:10, 15; 28:1) is not told us, for it does not affect the story. Since this migration ended in Canaan, the outsider, unaware of the inner spiritual motivation, is given that as the original purpose of leaving Ur.

Then we are introduced to the spiritual reality behind the externals. However little it might appear to the onlooker, however many other motives may have played a part, the inner drive of all that was happening came from God's call to Abram. Terah's actions were merely marginal.

It has often been suggested that Abram's faith influenced his father sufficiently for him to throw in his lot with his son. Then by the time they reached Haran, old age, weariness or decreasing faith caused him to abandon the seemingly endless journey. This is, of course, plausible and even "edifying", but it is pure conjecture based on silence and a feeling of what should have been.

It may be that archaeology by its interpretation of Abram the Hebrew (14:13) has suggested the answer. Conjecture it must remain, but at least it seems to be firmly anchored in what we know of the period. Whereas "Hebrew" used to be linked with Eber (10:24, 25), or interpreted as "the man from the other side", it is now linked by most with *habiru* and cognate terms found for over half a millennium in documents and inscriptions that have come down to us. The term occurs with varying shades of meaning over the centuries, wanderers, mercenaries, serfs, etc., but apparently always with the idea of less than full citizenship. Professor Albright argued persuasively that in the time of Abram it meant caravaneers, plying their trade with the aid of asses, which were only later replaced first by mules and then by camels. He has shown conclusively that much that is told us of Abram's moves in Canaan fits in with what is known of the caravan trade with Egypt round 2,000 B.C.[1]

If this is so, it explains much. Abram regarded Paddan-Aram, the area around Haran, as his native land (24:4, 10 – Nahor was near Haran). This frees us from thinking of Terah and his sons, Semites, as citizens of Sumerian Ur. They were there in the interests of the caravan trade, but they were only tolerated aliens and need not have lived within the city walls. When Abram told his father that he was going, Terah probably felt too old to carry on by himself in an alien setting. When he reached Haran he was not merely at home once again, but also in one of the major centres of the caravan trade. No wonder he stayed there.

It should be noted that all that is told us of Abram and his descendants fits in with this pattern. Except for Esau, they are never found far from human settlements, but they do not live in them. If Abram had 318 trained men available, when the four kings from Mesopotamia broke into Canaan (14:4), they will have been his caravaneers, whom he had

---

[1] Cf. W. F. Albright, *The Biblical Period from Abraham to Ezra*, pp. 5ff.

collected at Hebron until the troubles were past.

Down the centuries the words have resounded: "Leave your country, your kinsmen and your father's house for the country I will show you. I will make you a great nation; I will bless you and make your name great, so that you will be a blessing.

> I will bless those who bless you;
> I will curse those who make little of you and despise you;
> In you all families on earth shall be blessed."

God sent forth his Son, when the time had fully come (Gal. 4:4), and part of that fulness of time was the bringing of the lands round Palestine under a common culture and rule, which enabled the news of the Messiah to spread quickly. In the days of Abram there was no common rule in "the Fertile Crescent" from the Egyptian frontier to the Persian Gulf, but Akkadian, the language of Babylonia, was widely known by the educated throughout the area, and there was a similar culture and religious system. So while Abram was being called to go from all that was dear and familiar to him, he was not being asked to face the completely unknown.

God's demands on Abram were great, but within the limits he could bear. It is an illustration of the truth of Paul's saying, "God keeps faith, and he will not allow you to be tested above your powers" (1 Cor. 10:13, NEB). It is no chance that when he went to Egypt (12:10–20), with its very different culture, his faith cracked. There is, incidentally, no indication that God commanded him to go to Egypt. Both he and Isaac had a similar experience at Gerar (20; 26:6–11), an early Philistine settlement, where again the culture was an alien one. The missionary who outruns the call of God either does not really contact those to whom he has gone, or runs a serious risk of "cultural shock", the former being, of course, the far commoner today.

So the command "Leave" did not imply moving into a

sort of cultural vacuum, where he could make an entirely
new beginning, as the Pilgrim Fathers dreamt of doing
when they left for New England. It meant cutting himself
off from every form of human aid that might be provided
by past links and the demands of family relationship. God
was demanding complete trust in himself; Abram was not
to be granted even the choice of when and whither. In
return there was the promise that God would make him
become a great nation – not merely numerous but also
famous – that he would bless him and make his name great.

In an age in which religion has for so many become
marginal its vocabulary has become vague, and by many it
is considered pedantic to ask what its terms mean. That this
is true of "to bless" may be seen in some of the strange
utterances that pass for a benediction in these days. In
addition few ask themselves how man can be said to bless
God, who is the source of all true blessing.

There is little doubt that the Hebrew verb *barak*, to bless,
is linked with *berek*, a knee. When the greater gave to the
weaker and poorer, who was in need, the latter knelt before
him in gratitude with empty hands outstretched. This is
what God's blessing means, his gracious giving to the one
in need, whether this is material or spiritual. Man in return
blesses the giver, above all God, by his humble acknowledgement of need and grateful acceptance of what is given.
So God's statement that he would bless Abram implied that
all that he would give would be of grace, and that Abram's
greatness would be entirely of God's creating.

In theory a person's name was a true description or
reflection of his position and nature; it hardly needs saying
that it seldom worked out that way. Even so, to make a
person's name great implied that he would be famous for his
character and actions. From the sequel it is clear that next to
Jesus the Messiah and possibly Moses, Abraham ranks
higher than any other in the religious world's estimation, if
we look at the three main monotheistic religions. But this
greatness was not to be for his own self-aggrandizement but

that he might be a blessing to others. He was to receive
richly from God, that in turn he might pass on the divine
riches to others.

At least in its primary sense, "I will bless those that bless
you" is no mere promise of blessing to the philo-semite, to
the one who seeks to do good and show kindness to the Jew
for one reason or another. Yet we should not forget Matt.
25:40. In this setting to bless Abraham and his descendants
(not necessarily all Jews! – Rom. 4:16, Gal. 3:7) means
to accept gratefully and humbly that which God offers
through them. Let us not forget that there are many who
call themselves Christians, who resent it, when they are
reminded that according to the flesh Jesus was a Jew. Even
more of them, either deliberately or by neglect, try to
eliminate the revelation of the Old Testament from their
religion.

"I will curse those who make little of you and despise
you" is a rendering which tries to bring out the meaning of
the Hebrew. The traditional rendering, retained by RSV,
"him who curses you I will curse", ignores that the Hebrew
uses two different words of considerably different meaning.
"I will curse those who slight you" (JB) is better, but is too
weak; "those that curse you I will execrate" (NEB) is in
itself excellent, but it uses a term outside the vocabulary of
the average man.

We must face the added difficulty that while to curse
originally meant to call down divine vengeance on a person,
now, more often than not, it is used of rude and insulting
language. For the former sense we have four or five terms in
Hebrew, the most important being *'arar*; for the latter *qillel*,
literally to make light, is used. It is these two verbs we find
here. There are a few cases where *qillel* and its noun *qelalah*
approach the meaning of calling down a curse, but normally
to revile is nearer the meaning. Not so much the bitter
hatred of the antisemite is here envisaged but man's despis-
ing and dishonouring of Abraham's descendants.

It is worth mentioning that it is *qelalah* that is used in the

verse so much misused by antisemites and the like, viz.
Zech. 8:13. NEB tries to avoid the misunderstanding by
translating "symbol of a curse"; "a curse word" would have
been better.

"In you all families on earth shall be blessed"; such is the
rendering of all the early versions and most Jewish commentators – Rashi is a major exception – but modern translations favour "by you all the families of the earth shall bless
themselves", i.e., they shall say, "May I be blessed as
Abraham was". Obviously the difference in meaning is
small, but not unimportant. The modern rendering is
almost certainly correct in 22:18; 26:4, where a different and
indubitably reflexive form of the verb is used. The form
used in 12:3; 18:18; 28:14 could in theory be either passive or
reflexive. Unfortunately it is found only in these three
passages, so we cannot judge from its use elsewhere. Since
arbitrary verbal changes are not common in solemn promises, we shall do well to respect the difference and retain the
traditional rendering in these three passages. A possible
explanation for the change in 22:18; 26:4 is that not the
patriarch but only his descendants are mentioned, not all of
whom would necessarily prove a blessing.

Just as we are not told how long it took Abram to reach
Haran from Ur, so equally the length of the way from
Haran to Canaan remains unrecorded. It is the onward
march of faith that matters, not the length of the road it has
to traverse or the time involved. God waited until Abram
had reached Shechem, the natural heart of Canaan, before
He made known to him that at last he had reached his goal.

We then have the cryptic remark, "At that time the
Canaanites were in the land" (12:6). For over a century the
majority of Old Testament scholars have used this as a
proof that the story must have received its present form at a
time when the Canaanites were no more. Since the conquest
of Canaan was one of the outstanding memories of the
people, ranking with the Exodus and the giving of the Law
at Sinai, the logic of this deduction seems to be remarkably

weak. Far more likely is that we are to infer the shock caused
to Abram by God's declaration, "To your descendants I
will give this land" (12:7). It belongs to the nature of faith
that it looks away from the perils and difficulties that sur-
round it to God on high, even as Peter, when he walked the
waves of Gennesaret, had eyes only for his Lord (Matt.
14:28–31). Normally, however, there comes the moment
when the perils and difficulties become a reality; as with
Peter, they may deflect one's gaze from God. What Abram
had expected from God's call, we are not told, but it must
have come as a shock to him that the land to be inherited was
densely populated, at least in parts. That this is the correct
explanation of the remark about the Canaanites is suggested
by 13:7, where the mention of the Canaanites and Perizzites
is surely meant to explain why there was insufficient pasture
land for both Abram and Lot.

There is a tendency in some circles to separate the promise of the land in 12:7 from the initial promise at the time
of Abram's call. The purpose behind this separation is varied. There are those who genuinely feel that an essentially
spiritual promise cannot be permanently linked with a physical one, that the promise of the land was merely something
temporary to aid the achievement of the spiritual. Less
laudable is the attitude of those who maintain that the
promises to Abraham have not merely been enlarged to take
in his descendants through faith, but that they, i.e., the
Church, have taken them over, leaving nothing for the
Jews. Ever since the disastrous outcome of the Crusades the
churches have come to terms with reality and have claimed
only the "holy places" as their portion of the land. There are
yet others who are essentially swayed by their emotions.
They may seek to deny the land to the Jew out of sympathy
for the dispossessed Arabs, or out of anti-semitic dislike and
hatred, which demand that the Jew should pass through the
world without a home.

This process of separation has been aided by the tendence
of many to regard "To your descendants I will give this

land" as an essentially separate promise. But the very send-
ing of Abram to a specific land (12:1) was by inference the
promise of a land. It could not be specified and promised
until Abram, following God's leading in faith, had reached
it.

Those who find it hard to combine the spiritual and the
essentially physical, and they are many, have not grasped
the fact and mystery of "corporeality". They share in the
ancient error of many Greeks that matter is evil or at the best
something lower. The eternal Word of God became flesh
(Jn. 1:14) not merely for the salvation of man but also for the
reconciliation of heavenly as well as of earthly things (Col.
1:19). More than that, he has retained his risen, earthly,
material body for all eternity. It would seem to be God's
will that his purposes should be worked out through the
material. Just as the garden in Eden should have been gradually extended until it embraced the world, so Canaan should
have been the centre from which the knowledge of God
should have spread world wide, until the earth was full of
the knowledge of the Lord as the waters cover the sea. This
remains the Scriptural hope also in the New Testament.
Whereas Ezekiel saw in vision a small city named "The
Lord is there" (Ezek. 48:35), on the new earth in Rev. 21 it
has become a great mountain which fills the earth.

We are told that Abram marked the divine appearance
and promise at Shechem by the building of an altar. Though
it is not stated, it is reasonable to suppose that it was some
form of realisation of God's care and presence that caused
him to build his second altar between Bethel and Ai (12:8).
This latter altar is mentioned again in 13:4, after Abram's
safe return from the perils of Egypt. When he moved his
main centre to the vicinity of Hebron an altar is once again
mentioned (13:18). Apart from the much later building of
an altar at Mt Moriah, as a preparation for the sacrifice of
Isaac, we are told no more of the outward ritual of Abram's
worship.

An altar presupposes sacrifices, but we are told nothing of

them. There are good grounds for believing that there was not much difference between the sacrifices brought by the Patriarchs and those later enjoined by the Mosaic law, for these were all basically older than the Sinaitic covenant. What mattered was that the latter were God's command with even the smallest details laid down, while the former were the expression of the Patriarchs' spiritual needs and desires, which God in grace accepted, but which were not types and shadows from which the people of God should learn. Beyond a few special occasions we have no information about Abram's prayers, and of his worship we know only that he "invoked Jehovah by name" (12:8). On one occasion at least he brought tithes (14:20), almost certainly of the booty gained from his defeat of the four kings. Whether he did so on other occasions is not suggested, though it is likely that he did.

There are many today who lay very great stress on right theology and right worship, and who would dare say that they are wrong? Abraham, however, and for that matter Isaac and Jacob as well, stresses the primacy of a right relationship with God through faith. So long as we remember that it is not in Scripture, it probably matters little what theology and worship we attribute to Abraham. They were so insignificant compared with his faith that Scripture does not record them.

There are good grounds, supported by archaeology, for believing that Abram was what is technically called an ethical monotheist.[1] Having been brought up in the midst of polytheism and idolatry and having been surrounded by them in his father's home, he probably never doubted that these things had some form of real existence. But then Yahweh (Jehovah) – or did he call him El Shaddai, God Almighty, cf. Exod. 6:3? It matters not – revealed himself

---

[1] Cf. especially A. Alt, "The God of the Fathers" in *Essays on Old Testament History and Religion*, pp. 1–66, and W. F. Albright, *From the Stone Age to Christianity*, pp. 188f.

to him. We are not told how, because it belongs to the essence of the first steps of faith that they are something completely personal, that one man's experience cannot be the pattern for another's. But once the personal relationship had been established then Abram was prepared to follow and obey Jehovah alone, even though there might be many "gods" and many "lords" (1 Cor. 8:5).

This is why there is something so basic in Abram's story. Culture and nurture, environment and education, the differences between the extrovert and the introvert may deeply influence a man's understanding of God and the way in which he finds him or rather is found by him. To all, however, Abram says that it is a question of knowing God – not knowing about him – and of obeying Him.

Additional Note
The Rabbis and Abraham

The rabbis realized something of the greatness of Abraham and lovingly embroidered the biblical story, filling in what they felt were the gaps in the biblical narrative from their own imagination. This must have started early, for we have examples of it in the fragmentary *Genesis Apocryphon* from Qumran. Here we have space only for the tales how he came to faith in Jehovah.

His father Terah was not only an idolator, but he also sold idols. But even as a child Abram was dissatisfied. One night, as he looked at the stars, he felt, "These are the gods". But with the coming of dawn they faded from sight, so he transferred his veneration to the sun, but this in turn set, as did the moon which replaced it. So he decided that there must be one who was the creator of stars, sun and moon, who must be the true god.

One day, being left in charge of his father's shop, he took a hammer and broke pieces off the various images. Then he damaged the largest and placed the hammer in his mutilated arms. When his father came home and, horrified, asked what had happened, Abram explained that the gods had started quarrelling, so the largest took a hammer to keep them in order, and that he had caused all the damage. When his father angrily told him, "But there is no life or power in them to do such things", his young son retorted, "Why then do you serve them? Can they hear your prayers, when you call on them?"

Like all the other legends, the stories are attractive, but behind them we can see the Jew preaching monotheism to his pagan neighbours and confounding them by such arguments.

CHAPTER 4

ABRAHAM AND LOT
(*Gen. 13, 18*)

Since it always seems to afford a certain type of Christian a great deal of satisfaction, when he can find fault with the great men of the Bible, Lot has drawn more than his fair share of their fire. It is often suggested that, since God's call had come to Abram, Lot had no right to try and share in it. If anyone made a mistake, it was Abram not Lot, for it is clearly stated that it was Abram who took Lot with him (12:5). Though we cannot be certain what the basis for Abram's authority over his nephew may have been, the linking of him with Sarai suggests that it lay in the accepted rules of clan life at the time, cf. 11:31. That Lot was not opposed to going with his uncle is suggested by 12:4; 13:5.

Similarly, others have blamed Lot for separating from his uncle (13:11). They suggest that his "worldly-mindedness", which was to show itself later, made the influence of his "spiritually-minded" uncle unwelcome. The simple physical fact is that they had to separate. Even though Canaan was not as heavily populated as it was at the time of the Conquest we are reminded, "At that time the Canaanites and the Perizzites dwelt in the land" (13:7).

It has apparently been a feature of Palestinian life as far back as we can trace, that the nomad was welcome to graze the short-lived herbage of his settled neighbours and, it may be, the stubble after the harvest, which helped to manure the fields. The same principle accounts for Egypt's willingness to admit nomadic groups under certain circumstances. The degree to which this was possible depended on the size of the settled population at any given time, but obviously the number of the nomads and the size of their flocks and herds had to be strictly limited. If there is any moral at all in the separation, it is surely that riches acquired in Egypt bring few or no blessings with them.

Great stress is often laid on Abram's faith and generosity in giving his nephew a free choice which part of the land he would live in. In fact, it is difficult to see how a man of his character could have acted otherwise, the more so as the whole outlook of his time expected such an attitude from the elder and richer. He had caused his nephew to come this long way from whatever land he called home, and he could not leave him in the lurch.

Obviously God's promise to Abram, a reaffirmation of 12:7, once Lot had left him (13:14–17), is in measure a commendation of his action. Yet there is no suggestion that it was because of his faith. Rather it was because Abram had acted rightly and righteously. In Israel's ethics one sign of the truly godly man was that "he swears to his own hurt and does not change" (Psa. 15:4). Right or wrong, Abram had brought Lot with him and he was not going to back out of the consequences. In fact the spiritual lesson would seem to be that God will see to it that we shall not ultimately be the losers by doing that which is right and fair. Sometimes God gives even more than we abandon to others; sometimes it seems that we have lost by our generosity and right dealing. Always, however, there is the Divine blessing and providing.

There are many who blame Lot for his "selfish" choice. They are the type of people who give a child a bag of sweets and then tell him to offer them to the assembled company. They think little of his feelings as he sees them rapidly grow less, and above all his favourites vanishing fast. Abram's offer was genuine and what Lot chose coincided with his uncle's wish that he should really choose. It might even be

suggested that Lot, knowing that the land had been promised to his uncle, deliberately chose a relatively small and
marginal portion, however fertile, so as not to impinge
upon Abram and his descendants.

Though it has no bearing on the spiritual application of
the story, it is worth mentioning the problem of the site of
the cities of the plain. Today it is fairly generally accepted
that they were at the south end of the Dead Sea, and that
their ruins lie under the shallow waters. That is probably
why the Israelis have called their settlement there S'dom.
The mention in Gen. 14:3–10 is too vague for any deduction
to be drawn. Certainly, however, the south end of the sea
could not have been seen from Bethel (13:2), and it is
difficult to see how it could have been called, by any stretch
of imagination, "the Jordan valley" (13:10, 11). The same
inference that they must have lain at the north end of the sea
should be drawn from 18:16, if indeed it implies that they
could be seen from Hebron. So, in spite of the lack of any
archaeological discoveries, we would do well to think of
them as being at the north end of the Dead Sea.[1]

Then Lot is blamed for deliberately running himself into
temptation (13:13). This, however, assumes that the reputa-
tion of the cities of the plain was already known to Abram
and Lot. Indeed, had it been, we should rather blame
Abram for not warning his considerably younger nephew,
indeed for giving him such a free choice. The comment in
14:13, suggests that when Lot preferred Sodom, he was
already aware of the moral danger.

If we want to criticize Lot – why should we? – we should
do it on the basis of what the New Testament leaves unsaid
about him. He is called "righteous Lot, greatly distressed by
the licentiousness of the wicked" (2 Pet. 2:7). What is not
attributed to him is faith. In Heb. 11:9, 10 the faith that
marked out Abraham, Isaac and Jacob is seen especially in

---

[1] The arguments are summarized in George Adam Smith, *The Historical Geogra-
phy of the Holy Land*[23] pp. 505–508. NBD rejects a northern location but on
apparently inadequate arguments.

their willingness to do without the security offered by an earthly city and to live instead in tents. It is this faith that Lot evidently lacked and which caused him, once he did not have his uncle's support, first to move near Sodom and then to make his home there. He did not learn his lesson even when he was made a captive in war (14:12, 16).

By the time that Abraham was told by God of the coming judgment on the cities of the plain (18:17, 20) he was fully aware of the true situation. This is already implicit in his stinging snub of the king of Sodom (14:21–23), when he refused to profit from him in any way. So he did not misunderstand the force of God's words, when he said, "I will go down to see whether they have done altogether according to the outcry which has come to me; and if not, I will know". God was not suggesting that he did not know. Rather he was saying that, in an age in which gods were believed to act on passing whims, he would base his judgment on a judicial enquiry. That Abraham so understood it is shown by his basing his plea on the fact that God is "Judge of all the earth".

Abraham's prayer is frequently misunderstood and then misapplied. We read that "Abraham still stood before the Lord" (18:22). By ancient rabbinic tradition this is one of the *tiqqune sopherim*, i.e. deliberate scribal changes, made mostly for reverential reasons, the original being "the Lord still stood before Abraham"; few scholars doubt that this was the original. It implies that God was waiting for Abraham to open his heart to him.

God was not inviting Abraham to change his mind by prayer; rather he was giving him the opportunity of understanding God's mind and nature through prayer. Abraham was really praying for Lot rather than Sodom – there is no suggestion that he was concerned about the other cities of the plain. If he ever doubted Lot's safety, he very soon lost his fear as he spoke to the universal and all-righteous Judge. But he was still concerned for Lot's possessions, his comfort, his standing in society. The saving of Sodom would mean the saving of all this for his nephew. But as he increased his demands by lessening the number of righteous needed, he evidently realized more and more the implications of his request.

Self-righteous Christians often blame him for stopping at ten righteous. He should have gone on they say. Far from it! He knew full well that Lot and his family accounted for four of the needed total. If these four had not been able to win over six more during the passing years, then the situation of Sodom must be desperate, and it had become a plague spot, which threatened the whole of Canaan. He was right; there are things we cannot ask for without flouting God's moral government.

The final pages in Lot's life bear out the comment made earlier. Though he knew that God's hand had been over him to save him, he still could not rely on God's protection. He had to have the safety of a fortified community, however small, and so saved Bela, or Zoar, from destruction at that time (19:18–22).

We find the behaviour of Lot's daughters disgusting, and yet they showed more faith than their father. He, stripped of ambitions, wife, home and possessions, could not see God's hand in his survival and was prepared to end his days as a pauper, skulking in a mountain cave. The girls realized that their survival was a clear sign of God's grace and were determined to live on for future generations, even if the means they chose would under normal circumstances have carried the death penalty with it. Lot had left Zoar, for its inhabitants feared that he carried the curse that had overwhelmed the cities. That is a perfectly adequate explanation why the girls knew they could not find husbands. Yet we may perhaps see in their action that they were answering local fear and rejection by an even more radical rejection. It was their declaration that they knew the available young men were as worthy of death as the two to whom they had been engaged, and so they would have none of them.

We may well ask, why Lot did not turn to his uncle in the

hour of disaster. The obvious answer is that a younger man who has thrown away prosperity and property very often shrinks from turning to the older and prosperous, lest he should say, "I told you so". This probably played a part, but we ought to look deeper.

It is remarkable that in the story of Abram's victory over the five confederate kings (14:13–24), which resulted in Lot being freed and having his property restored, there is not a word said of what may have passed between uncle and nephew. This must not be overstressed, because the centre of the stage is held by Abram and Melchizedek, and the whole chapter seems to come from a non-Israelite source.[1] For all that the silence conforms to much human experience.

For the worldling the man of faith seldom creates much ill-feeling; he tends to be regarded as not a little mad, and his prosperity, if it is there, can be explained away as chance. The God-fearing man, however, who walks in the light of worldly wisdom, finds the man of faith a continual rebuke, and detests it, when the latter's success rebukes his manner of life. Had Lot returned to Abram, it would have been a tacit acknowledgement that he had been right all along, and he could have found no valid reason for not joining him in his walk of faith.

As the curtain falls on Lot in his poverty and shame, it rises on Abraham seeing the beginning of God's fulfilment of his promises, not so much in his prosperity, but rather in the gift, at long last, of the son through whom the promises would pass on to later generations. This was underlined by God's giving him a new name, changing Abram to Abraham, even as he changed Sarai to Sarah (17:5, 15).

It is usual to stress the change in meaning between Abram and Abraham, but since there is no discernable difference in meaning between Sarai and Sarah, we may question whether the difference between Abram = Exalted Father

---

[1] Cf. Speiser, *Genesis* (Anchor Bible), pp. 108f.

and Abraham = Father of a Multitude (of nations) lies only
in the meaning. Let the reader remember that in Hebrew the
final syllable is strongly accented, and that in addition the *H*
is clearly pronounced. If he will then utter both names
loudly and clearly, he will realize that God was now giving
his servant a name that demanded respect, as he was introduced into the presence of the great men of the earth.
Something of the respect with which he came to be
regarded may be seen in 23:6. So over against Lot's shame
we can place the honour given to the man who was prepared
to trust his God completely.

CHAPTER 5

THE BINDING OF ISAAC
(*Gen. 22*)

The binding of Isaac, or '*aqedah*, as it is usually called by the religious Jew, has played a major part in the piety of the Synagogue down the centuries. At the first the stress may have been in conscious opposition to Christianity, but if this is so, it must have begun early; already in Dura Europos on the Euphrates we find the scene depicted on the wall of a ruined synagogue built about the middle of the third century A.D. The mosaic showing the same scene from the ruins of the synagogue at Beit Alpha, some three centuries later, is known to most visitors to Israel, who are interested in its antiquities.

In contrast to the average Christian picture Isaac is depicted as a full grown young man. Indeed, already Josephus (*Ant.* I. xiii. 2) states that he was twenty-five at the time, while *Jubilees*, not later than 100 B.C., and possibly a century earlier, makes him twenty-three (17:15). Behind such estimates must lie reasonable deductions from the fact that Isaac was able to carry the wood for the burnt-offering up the hill (22:6) and even more the realization that the sacrifice derived its full value from the fact that Isaac accepted God's will as well as his father. The estimate of thirty-seven given by *Seder Olam*[1] is clearly based on the

---

[1] The *Seder Olam*, from the late third century A.D. gives the rabbinic interpretation of Old Testament chronology. It has no authority.

supposition that Sarah's death (23:1) took place immediately afterwards, which is most improbable.

Clearly, God spoke to Abraham at night (cf. v. 3). It makes little difference whether it was in a dream, or whether like Samuel he was wakened from sleep by the divine voice. It was about fifty years since Abraham had left Haran in obedience to the voice of God. He had made his mistakes and had thought that the voice of his own desires represented the will of God. Now he knew better and made no effort to dodge the command as it came remorselessly to his inner ear.

"Abraham" – this was something for him and for him alone; something he and no other could carry out.

"Here am I" – this is the answer of the ready and obedient servant; the master has only to command and he will obey.

"Take your son" – the Hebrew by adding *na'* turns the apparent command into a request, though to render it by "please" would be unduly to weaken it. God is making his will quite clear, but he also indicates that he will understand, if Abraham considers its burden too great.

"Your only one" – but Ishmael was also his son, the only one of his mother; "whom you love" – but Abraham loved them both; "Isaac" – now there was no longer any doubt, and we are told that "he rose early in the morning", for the will of God does not become easier as we put off doing it.

We are told that God tested Abraham – the AV rendering "tempted" meant exactly the same at the time it was made – and something in most of us rebels at the thought of the old man having to suffer like this. The simple and inexorable fact is that in the physical, mental and spiritual realms alike, we cannot tell how much value to give to a claim until it has been tested. Abraham had proclaimed his complete faith in God, but if he was in fact to become the father of all who believe, the reality of his faith had to be shown beyond a doubt.

"Go into the land of Moriah" – in 2 Chr. 3:1 the Temple hill is called Mt Moriah, but no attempt is made to link it with Abraham's sacrifice. Doubtless this identification had been made by the Chronicler's time, while the Samaritans claimed that Shechem was indicated. The name is otherwise unknown to us, and archaeology has not helped in its identification. The Genesis story is deliberately vague, for God was not seeking to create a holy place out of Abraham's suffering and obedience. If pious imagination links the place of Abraham's sacrifice with Golgotha, no harm is done, provided we realize that it is the act and not the site which is of importance. So let it be Jerusalem for our present purpose.

Abraham slipped off early with Isaac and two servants. This was not merely for the reason suggested earlier. He wanted to avoid awkward questions from Sarah. It would be bad enough to return to her without Isaac; it would be almost more than flesh and blood could bear to be pursued by her lamentations, and in any case he did not want the purpose of the journey revealed to his son in this way.

Slowly they trudged along the old road that came out of Egypt and after passing through Beer-sheba ran northwards past Hebron, Jerusalem and Shechem until it joined the *Via Maris*, the main trade route to the Euphrates. When they came to a suitable place they cut enough wood for the sacrifice, for even in those days Canaan in many of its parts, especially in the south, was short of trees.

We may picture the three young men happily exchanging news with the caravans they passed. They were young, without a care and on the high road. They will hardly have noticed that Abraham was strangely silent. There will have been a pause during the midday heat, and then the road led ever northwards until they camped for the night.

The young men were soon tight asleep, enjoying the rest of youth, but old Abraham by the fire, kept burning to frighten away wild animals, was sunk in thought. The voice that had been dogging him all day became clearer. "Abraham, you poor fool. Did I not warn you in Ur, in Haran, that you could not trust El Shaddai. I told you that he was merely leading you by the nose, to leave you in the lurch at the last. You thought you had everything, when he gave you Isaac, and now in a few hours you will have nothing. Poor fool!"

He lifted his eyes to the stars above him. Years earlier God had called him out of his tent and told him to look up at the stars (15:5). As many as the stars in heaven would his descendants be. He had believed, and his God had reckoned it to him as righteousness. That night heaven had seemed so near, and the stars looked like holes poked by angel fingers in the vault of heaven to let the glory of heaven shine through, but now they seemed cold, far away and mocking.

So the night passed and a new day came. They were soon on their way again ever northwards. Hebron with its well-known faces was behind them. Probably he had had to stop and introduce his son to old friends, while all the time his heart was bleeding. And so at last the second night came, and once again there were three asleep and one awake. This time it is Abraham that sleeps and Isaac watches.

New thoughts had come to the old man during the day. He looked back on the many years of obedient following, and repeatedly he had to confess that God had been as good as his word, better than Abraham had ever expected. So insistently the question presented itself: why should God be different now? Why? More than that – Isaac was a miracle child. If God could give them a child when all natural hope was long past, did he not have the power to give back life too. Resurrection from the dead was something no one had experienced, but why should the Lord of life not be able to do even this? "He considered that God was able to raise men even from the dead" (Heb. 11:19), and so with lighter heart he slept before the crisis of the morrow.

For Isaac the novelty of the journey had worn off and he had more time to think of its purpose and of his father's strange silence. Sacrifice was an occasion for joy, but there was no joy here. All that was necessary for the offering had been prepared except the victim. True enough, a sacrificial animal could easily be bought in one of the places they had to pass, but yet there was something strange, inexplicable. So we can picture the feeling stealing over him that he was destined to be the offering.

Until recently it was generally accepted that human sacrifice was a commonplace in Bible lands, and so both Abraham and Isaac were well acquainted with the custom. The archaeologist now informs us that the custom was extremely rare, the chief exception being the Phoenician practice of passing children through the fire "to Moloch", which had a stronger and more continuing life in Carthage. There is not much evidence for its practice among the Canaanites generally. To be noted is that it would seem that it was mainly little children that were involved, and at least in Phoenicia the sacrifice was resorted to only in times of major crisis, cf. 2 Ki. 3:26, 27. So both Abraham and Isaac, while they could not see any reason, must have envisaged a major motivation for God's demand.[1]

With this in mind we may imagine Isaac praying by the camp fire. "O God, God of my father Abraham, thou hast given me life; thou hast promised that through me thy blessing will pass on to the world. I do not know thee as my father does; I have not served thee as he has, and yet I must trust thee and obey thee. If I am to be the sacrifice, I do not understand thy will. I am afraid, and yet I am willing, if only for my father's sake".

And so the third morning came. They crossed the shoulder of the hill near where later Bethlehem was to stand, and before them lay the little Jebusite town of Urusalim, where once Abraham had been greeted by Melchizedek. Then God said, "You are nearly there, Abraham". They passed under the shadow of the walls as they mounted the Kidron ravine. Abraham said to his servants, "This will do, lads. The sacrifice concerns only Isaac and me. Stay here with the donkey, while we go over there". There was a moment's

[1] Cf. R. de Vaux, *Ancient Israel*, pp. 441–446, *Studies in Old Testament Sacrifice*, pp. 52–90; W. F. Albright, *Yahweh and the Gods of Canaan*, pp. 203–212.

hesitation; then with the full, clear certainty of victorious faith he added, "We shall come again to you".

Father and son climb the hill in silence in the early morning light. Isaac bowed under the weight of the wood, Abraham with the knife and fire. Isaac decided that the time had come for certainty. "Father!";

"Yes, my boy."

"Here are wood and fire, but where is the lamb?"

"My boy, God will provide himself a lamb for a burnt offering."

Isaac looked at his father and said, "I understand, and I am ready". So the heaviest burden rolled from Abraham's heart.

The final preparations cannot have lasted long. Rough stones soon made an altar on which the wood could be laid. Then Abraham tied Isaac's legs together. The verb *'aqad*, used only here, would seem to be a technical term for tying up an animal for sacrifice. Isaac was to be treated in all things as though he were a sacrificial animal, for otherwise there would have been no point in the binding. Isaac could almost certainly have resisted his father, and quite certainly could have run away. He was acting like a much greater sacrifice, of whom it was foretold that he would be "like a lamb that is led to the slaughter".

Abraham had picked up the knife to complete the sacrifice, when the Angel of the Lord, God himself, called "Abraham, Abraham". So close had Isaac come to death, so concentrated was Abraham's mind on his terrible task, that nothing less than the double call could break through to his consciousness. Almost mechanically the answer comes, "Here am I". The voice continued, "Do not raise your hand against the boy; do not touch him. Now I know that you are a God-fearing man".

"Now I know" – surely God had known it all along, and the only one who might have been surprised at the successful end of the test was Abraham himself. That is of course true, but it is not the whole truth. When God handed Job over to the power of Satan, it was more than a test of Job's faith; it was also a demonstration to Satan of Job's loyalty and faith. Similarly Paul tells us "that through the church the manifold wisdom of God might now be made known to the principalities and powers in the heavenly places" (Eph. 3:10). There are spiritual beings who do not have merely to accept God's statements about men, but who see them borne out by the facts of their behaviour. The painful testing and manifold sufferings of God's people here on earth have a wider meaning than we can know down here.

Abraham stood there as a God-fearing man. At least three things conspire to make it very difficult for us to understand what is meant by the fear of the Lord. The advance of the physical sciences has largely stripped man of his sense of awe as he deals with God's creation and hence of a sense of awe as he faces the Creator. The rise of the United States of America and the French Revolution have so impressed us with a sense of man's equality, that respect for one's fellowman and then for his Creator have largely vanished. The revelation of the incredible love of God as revealed in Jesus the Messiah has to a great extent been debased by our common debasing of the term love itself. The God-fearer is one with a true vision both of God and man and is able to bring them both into true perspective. The man who had pleaded for Sodom (Gen. 18:22–32) was not afraid of God, but he was keenly aware of the true relationship between man and God.

We may picture Abraham with tear-filled eyes hardly able to see to undo the rope that bound Isaac, and then they were wrapped in one another's arms.

Suddenly Isaac said, "Father, do you see what I see?"

"Yes, surely I do".

"But where has it come from? It was not here while we were preparing for the sacrifice".

"Ah, my boy, didn't I tell you that God would provide the lamb for the burnt offering? Only he has done even more; it is a fine ram."

As Abraham and Isaac knelt beside the altar and watched the smoke of the sacrifice ascend to God a stranger might have said to them, "A strange God is this God of yours; why has he played such tricks on you?" Assuredly they would have answered, "Sir, we have suffered more than you can imagine, but in our suffering we have come to know our God more than you can imagine. It was terrible while it lasted, but it was abundantly worth it". Ever since, similar words have been used by those who have had to suffer, though normally in less degree.

The story ends with God swearing by himself to accomplish all that he had previously promised Abraham. In all the previous promises there had been the implied condition that Abraham would have to show trust and obedience. Now there was no need for any implied conditions, for it had been triumphantly demonstrated that trust and obedience were there in full measure, and so the promises were made absolute.

No attempt has been made to handle the story typologically. Provided the reality of Abraham's testing, and for that matter Isaac's, is not overlooked the reader may indulge himself.

Some little effort was made to bring out the reality of the three days journey from Beer-sheba to the place of sacrifice. Let us try to realize the burden not of three days but of thirty-three years both on Father and Son, as the shadow of the cross grew ever heavier, and both knew that it was to be no picture death and resurrection that lay ahead but the grimmest reality. He bore our sins in his own body right up to the tree, and God was in Christ reconciling the world to himself.

CHAPTER 6

"ISAAC TREMBLED EXCEEDINGLY"
(Gen. 32)

We sometimes meet admirable persons who make little or no impact on us until we see them in the context of other people. This is often due to physical weakness. Isaac seems to have been such a person. For this there is good reason.

God did not merely choose Israel to be his people; he made it. The birth of Isaac was miraculous – only the birth of the world's Redeemer was more so – so as to be an indication that God was beginning something new. This was confirmed by his being returned to his father, as if by a resurrection from the dead. Though it is nowhere explicitly stated, it is fairly clearly hinted that this outstanding example of God's sovereignty was made even clearer by Isaac's relative physical weakness, something that could in any case be expected of the child of aged parents. On the other hand the twenty years' wait before his sons were born (Gen. 25:20, 26) need not be attributed to physical incapacity. It can equally well be interpreted as a sign that not merely the beginning of Israel but also its continuance depended upon God.

Rebekah's delight, when she found that God had heard her husband's prayer and she was pregnant, soon changed to dismay when the twins in her womb seemed to be fighting. Her dismay was expressed by her incoherent cry, "If so, why I?" (25:22), for it could seem to be a withdrawal of the Divine favour. In her distress she went to inquire of

Jehovah. We are given no details of how or where, but the answer was clear. The two babes were to be the fathers of two nations very different in their natures. The struggle in her womb portended their future struggle and that of their descendants in which the younger would triumph. It is hardly credible that Rebekah did not share the oracle with her husband.

When the time came for the babies to be born, the first to emerge must have been a comic sight, dark reddish brown hair covering him all over. It was natural that he was called Esau, the hairy one. As the midwife tried to lift him she found that the second baby was holding him by the heel; so he in turn was called Jacob (*ya'aqob,* linked with *'aqeb,* heel). Because of what was to happen later, it is worth mentioning that this name was quite neutral. Indeed, it is possible that it meant "May he (God) be at your heels", i.e. be your defending rearguard, for archaeology knows such names in other Semitic languages, including a Ya'qub-ilu, i.e., May God be at his heels, from a Babylonian tablet from the time of Abraham.

The popular idea that the name means *deceiver* or *supplanter* (RV, mg.) is so implausible as to need no refutation. It is based on Esau's bitter cry in 27:36. One who catches you by the heel and throws you can well take advantage of the fact, and it may well be that Jacob himself came to understand his name like that (see next chapter), but basically the meaning has been imported from the way that Jacob behaved.

Extreme hairiness is popularly considered to be a sign of virility and strength; more often than not this is a superstition, but sometimes it is true, and so it was in Esau's case. We must think of the two boys growing up, Jacob slightly built, like the average Semite, but very tough, Esau a mountain of a man. Esau soon showed his liking for a wild and solitary life as he became "skilful in hunting, a man of the open plains" (NEB). Jacob, as the sequel shows, became a skilful shepherd, happiest when his tasks allowed him the

shelter of the family tent at night; Gen. 31:40 reminds us
that this could not always be taken for granted.

To this is added the statement that he was an *'ish tam*. This
has been a major problem for the translator. The Hebrew is
simple enough. By analogy with other passages, e.g. Gen.
6:9, Job 1:1, it should have been rendered "a perfect man"
(AV, RV), or better "a blameless man" (Moffatt, RSV,
NEB), but this stuck in the translators' throats, for they
could not bring themselves to say this of Jacob. AV, RV
"plain" means simple or honest; RV, mg., Moffatt, RSV,
JB, TEV suggest "quiet", with the alternative "harmless"
in RV, mg. "Jacob lived a settled life" (NEB) and "Jacob
was a retiring man who kept to his tents" (Speiser) are
presumably paraphrases of "quiet", but how suitable are
they for a Palestinian shepherd? Behind all these desperate
translational efforts lie partly an inherited bias against Jacob,
partly a failure to realize adequately that words like perfect
and blameless must in a book like the Bible be interpreted in
their setting, which is here a comparison with Esau, the
wild hunter. The root of *tam* means to be complete. Jacob
was a complete man, all sides of his personality developed,
in contrast to his brother who was all muscle and physical
desire.

We now meet the strange statement, "Isaac loved Esau,
because he ate of his game" – venison is more specific than
the Hebrew warrants. There is no evidence elsewhere that
Isaac was one of those gluttons whose god is their stomach.
In any case the sequel reveals that Rebekah was quite capable of making a dish out of a home-grown animal as tasty
as any meat brought home by Esau. Very often some food
or drink has a symbolic meaning for many, and we must
assume that the game stood for all that Esau was in Isaac's
eyes. All too often fathers allow some quality which they
miss in themselves but find in one of their children to cause
them to overvalue that son or daughter. If Isaac was com-
paratively weak, Esau's bulk, strength and hunting skill
provided a compensation for his own failings and caused

him to shut his eyes to his equally obvious faults. "But Rebekah loved Jacob" is the natural and inevitable corollary, the more so as Esau almost certainly used his superior strength to bully his brother.

Little harm would have been done, had not Isaac, quite obviously, persuaded himself that his wife had misunderstood the oracle and that Abraham's blessing was to be continued through Esau. God had been quite fair. He willed that through Jacob the blessing should be passed on, but Esau would have the birthright. Isaac hinted what he would do, while Rebekah and Jacob planned how to accomplish God's will, holding, as they obviously did, the popular maxim, "God helps those who help themselves".

Let any who are anxious to criticize and condemn them, pause a moment. The blessing, which God had given to Abraham and his descendants was something under God's control. He had passed over Ishmael, the first-born, to confer it on Isaac. The oracle had implied in reasonably unambiguous language that once again it was to come to the younger. It was clearly something that belonged to Jacob, and Rebekah and her younger son considered that Isaac's clearly suggested intention was nothing less than blatant robbery. What would their critics do, if they were faced with a comparable position, especially, if there were no court of law to turn to? Their critics will indubitably answer that they should have trusted God. Of course they should, but the many controversies about church property and funds – surely God's property! – which have come before secular courts show how easy it is to say what is right, and how hard it often is to do it.

The day came when their planning began to bear fruit. One day Esau came home from his hunting, tired, famished and apparently empty-handed. By strange coincidence there squatted Jacob cooking a rich red soup, which smelt delicious – had Rebekah given her son some cookery hints? Esau said to him, "Let me swallow some of the red, this red, for I am exhausted." "Certainly," said Jacob, "if you will

sell me your birthright for it." "Certainly," said Esau,
"what is the use of a birthright, if one is dying?" So Esau
sold his birthright, confirming it with an oath, and had his
soup with bread thrown in. The comment is, "Thus Esau
despised his birthright".

Most readers react violently. The opinion of many of
Jacob and his meanness can hardly be reproduced here. Let
them think a second time. Esau did not come across Jacob
somewhere in the wild but by the family tents. Dying of
hunger is a slow process and within half an hour he could
have had a square meal. The enigmatic way in which Esau
asked for the soup (masked by the standard translations)
reveals what really lay behind the incident. Esau did not
think of lentils, when he saw the rich red soup. He must
have thought it was blood soup with magical virtues, and
was doubtless intended to – this was before the Mosaic
legislation. The Noachic prohibition of the use of blood for
food (9:4), if not forgotten, was probably widely ignored.
One feature of the magic was that the name of the vital
element should not be mentioned.

The mocking nickname, Edom (Red), doubtless used
behind his back, shows that there was more in the incident
than Jacob's taking advantage of Esau's physical passions.
What deception there was lay in his getting what he asked
for but not what he expected. Heb. 12:16 holds up Esau as
the example of the immoral or irreligious man who sold his
birthright for a single meal. We may, however, well stop
and ask ourselves, whether he would have done it, had his
father not told him that he would be giving him something
far more precious. With a man like Esau it is impossible to
tell, but the possibility must not be dismissed out of hand.

The years passed and Isaac's sight failed him. Though he
was to live on for many years yet, this premature blindness
(he is the only comparable biblical character of whom it is
recorded) made him fear that he would die, his duty
unfinished. An old man making up his mind to do some-

thing big and decisive rarely finds it easy to hide his excitement; so when Esau came at his father's summons, Rebekah was hiding behind the tent curtains to discover what was exciting her husband. Obviously Isaac could have blessed him then and there, but he wished to make the ceremony as formal as possible. Perhaps, too, he thought that the game would silence the last nagging doubt at the back of his mind.

This was the moment Rebekah and Jacob had feared and discussed over the years. Her husband was now going to pass on the precious blessing to the wrong brother, even though it was God's will, clearly expressed before his birth, that Jacob should have it. She and her son were representative of so many, then and now, who sincerely accept God's will, yet cannot trust him to carry his will through. There are so many who sincerely believe that they, or others, are indispensable, if God's purposes are to be fulfilled.

An urgent message brought Jacob hurrying to his mother. "The moment has come; we must act now, while your brother is out hunting". Two kids and their skins and Esau's best clothes would be enough to deceive an old man, who had allowed his senses to be the interpreters of God's will to him.

Once again we are repelled by the apparent cynicism of Jacob's protest, "I shall seem to him a deceiver; and I shall bring a curse upon me" (27:12, RV). He does not mind deceiving, providing he is not found out; he is afraid of his father's curse, but not of God. But this is to misinterpret what he really said. Jacob said to himself that the blessing was his and therefore underhand means to obtain his own could hardly be called deceit. What he said to his mother was, "I shall seem to be mocking him" (RV, mg., Moffatt, RSV – not NEB, JB, TEV). None of those involved, except perhaps Esau, really believed that a blessing bestowed in God's name bound God's hands, if it were against his will, though a father's curse would be a heavy load. To steal such a blessing could bring no blessing with it. But Isaac had so convinced himself that Esau was the man of God's choice, that if he found another presenting himself, he would regard it as a mockery of a sacred task entrusted to him, rather than an effort to deceive.

Rebekah's answer, "Upon me be your curse, my son", has by some been compared with Lady Macbeth's, "But screw your courage to the sticking-place, and we'll not fail". There is, however, a nobility about it that is often missed. A knowledge of Abraham's response to God's call had lived on in the family of Nahor, and we gain the impression in Gen. 24 that when Rebekah enthusiastically accepted her place as Isaac's wife it was with the consciousness that she would be filling a place in God's purpose. Over the years she must have tried hard to bring Isaac round to a recognition of God's will. Now that the crisis had come, she was prepared to pay the price, provided God's will was done.

Rebekah's stratagem worked. For a moment Isaac was puzzled. The voice was wrong, but the hair, the smell, the food, the wine were right, and so he poured out his soul in blessing for the good gifts of the earth, for earthly power and for God's favour.

Jacob had hardly time to leave his father's tent, his purpose accomplished, before Esau returned to the encampment. The suggestion is less that of a narrow squeak and more of God's sovereignty using the mistaken efforts of Rebekah and Jacob. An hour or less later, while his father was still in the happy stupor of digestion, he was disturbed by Esau's voice, "Come, father; eat some of your son's game, that you may bless me". "Who are you?" We can catch the growing perplexity in the answer, "I am your son, your first-born, Esau." Surely his father was not so senile that he had forgotten what had been arranged only that morning.

We are told, "Then Isaac trembled greatly", and this is the clue to much in the story. However much we may criticize Isaac, he remains one of the heroes of faith. The relative passivity of his life and bodily weakness had predis-

posed him to being influenced by his surroundings, by the
impact of physical impressions, yet behind all was the desire
to do God's will. There must have been many moments
when he wondered whether his wife was not right after all.
Esau's loss of the birthright must have shaken him for a
while. Now suddenly he knew – he had no doubt that it was
Jacob that had come to him (v. 35) – and he bowed to God's
will. Not all Esau's tears could move him. Though he spoke
of Jacob's guile (v. 35), there is no evidence that he ever
reproved him, or Rebekah either, and he was prepared to
bless him again, knowingly and willingly (28:1–4).

Esau could see no further than the physical and so he had
no understanding of the spiritual mystery of the blessing.
Surely there must be one for him as well. Jacob, the heel-
man, had twice gripped him by the heel and thrown him.
He chose to forget that he had thrown his birthright away,
and he probably never grasped that the blessing was never
intended for him. So he wept and insisted.

Isaac knew that a purely human blessing was an empty
form of words. The spiritual blessing was Jacob's, and Esau
had thrown away the physical blessing of the birthright for
a few minutes of self-gratification, so there was nothing he
could give him. So when Esau insisted he gave him something that sounded fine but was hollow, AV, RV, tx. have
been misled by the ambiguity of the Hebrew – as Esau also
may have been for the moment? Modern versions give the
sense but not the ambiguity:

> Far from the richness of the earth shall be your dwelling,
> far from the dew of heaven above.
> By your sword shall you live,
> and you shall serve your brother.

The ambiguity simply cannot be indicated in English. It
comes from the use of *min* in the Hebrew of vv. 28, 39. In
the former it means a share of the natural blessings there
enumerated, in the latter a separation from them.

Even the final comment is full of ambiguity. "The time will come when you grow restive and break off his yoke from your neck." To cast off the yoke of the one chosen by God meant ultimate destruction, and freedom gained by force of arms would ultimately bring a curse with it.

There remained only one thing for Esau, revenge. We are told that he said to himself that his father would soon die, and then he would kill Jacob. A man like Esau cannot keep his mouth shut for long. Soon what was decided in his mind was blurted out to others and was by them repeated to Rebekah. The very fact that both mother and son never doubted that Esau could and would carry out his threat is sufficient evidence of Esau's superior strength. Since they had not trusted God to give what he had promised, there was also no trust there that God could and would keep the man of his choice. So Jacob had to learn among strangers that personal cleverness and wisdom would not work out God's plans.

CHAPTER 7

BETH-EL AND PENI-EL
(Gen. 28, 32)

The sun's rim was just touching the waters of the Great Sea
to the west as a man in shepherd's dress trudged along the
rough road to the height where stood the small town of Luz
on its *tel*.[1] He turned and looked south along the road to
Jerusalem and satisfied himself that there was no sign of his
being followed. He then looked over to the single gate of
Luz, where its guardians were preparing to close it before
darkness fell. "I do not want to be caught like a rat in a
trap," he said to himself and looked around for a sheltered
spot where he could spend the night.

Jacob was accustomed to sleeping rough, when he was
out with his sheep, so with a suitable stone as pillow and his
shepherd's cloak wrapped around him he was soon sleeping
the sleep of exhaustion. It was the second, if not the third,
night since he had left his father's tents near Beer-sheba.
Though he had gone at his mother's wish (Gen. 27:42–45)
and with his father's blessing (28:1–4), he had left as though
the hounds of hell were at his heels, for his conscience
imagined a vengeful Esau hunting him down. Only now
could he sleep quietly with a confidence that he had really
escaped the danger that threatened his life.

---

[1] *tel* in Hebrew means a mound, and it is used for those man-made mounds which
hide the remains of ancient cities. At all times the ground-level of inhabited
places rises, but when from the first they were built on hills, the result is a
mound easily recognizable by the trained eye.

Suddenly in a dream he found himself bathed in a light which showed him a ladder stretching from the place where he lay right into heaven. (The suggestion that the local rock-formation lay behind his dream may well be correct, but it is irrelevant.) As he watched he became aware of God's angels ascending and descending on the ladder. For most of us the story is so familiar that we do not recognize the strangeness of the language. Any normal child, in retelling the story, would make the angels come down before they mounted up again. This abnormal order is preserved in Jn. 1:51.

It was just this reversal of the normal that was a revelation to Jacob. Suddenly he realized that all the time he had been planning, toiling, deceiving, the angels of God had been around him, protecting him and leading him to the accomplishment of God's purposes, even though it had been along crooked ways of his own choosing and making. They had been with him also on his flight from home, and after reporting to their Master they had returned to go with him on his further way.

As this humiliating yet comforting fact sank into his consciousness, the Glory at the head of the ladder seemed to descend it and stand by him and speak to him, "I am Jehovah, the God of Abraham, your father, and the God of Isaac". This was the guarantee to Jacob that he stood firmly in the succession of the purposes of God and his salvation. The linking of "your father" with Abraham rather than with Isaac probably stresses less the priority of Abraham in God's purposes and more that Isaac's misunderstanding of God's will had not compromised Jacob's standing in the working out of God's purposes. Then God renewed the promises of blessing and of the land to Jacob and his descendants (verses 13–15). Finally there came the promise of the divine presence, protection and carrying out of his purposes.

Silence fell, the light vanished, and Jacob woke with a start. Trembling with awe he said, "This is a terrifying

place, the very house of God (Beth-el)". He lay awake until
the first light of dawn showed in the east. He rose swiftly,
not now because he feared that Esau might come, but
because the fear of the presence of God was upon him. He
up-ended the stone that had served as his pillow and
anointed it with oil, so as to mark for all who passed by, that
a theophany – a divine revelation, had taken place there. It is
clear that the inhabitants of Luz so understood it, for centuries later, after the conquest, Israel was able to claim the
site as one of its chief sanctuaries. For the polytheist it was
not important which god had claimed a few square yards of
earth by his presence, but they recognized that they had
been so claimed and thus rendered holy.

Before he went on his way, Jacob made a solemn promise. If God's promise should prove true, and he experienced God's presence in going, in sojourning and in returning, then Jehovah, and Jehovah alone would be his God, i.e.
he would acknowledge that Jehovah alone was the source of
all power. He would recognize in Beth-el his centre for
worship, and he would express both his dependence and his
gratitude by the giving of tithes.

Repeatedly Jacob has been criticized for his vow. We are
asked to recognize the old schemer as he tries to drive a
bargain with God. In all too many circles we are invited to
show our superiority over him, by omitting, when we sing
"O God of Bethel" its last verse,

> "Such blessings from Thy gracious hand
>   Our humble prayers implore;
> And Thou shalt be our chosen God,
>   And portion evermore."

Quite apart from the fact that Jacob could hardly have
believed that his tithes would mean so much to God, that he
could buy his favour by offering them – if we are to believe
what some Christians say, they do believe this! – we must
not forget his position. His grandfather had begun the

pathway of faith, but he cannot have been much more than a memory of a very old man, for Jacob was fifteen, when he died at the ripe old age of a hundred and seventy-five. Isaac, however, had done his best to frustrate the divine purpose, so there was far more excuse for any doubts that Jacob may have felt than there is for most of us. Quite apart from that, we must recognize that our prayers are very often on the same level.

Jacob stayed twenty years in Haran with Laban (31:41). Little that is told of him during this time throws much light on his attitude towards God. Clearly he still believed that God helps those that help themselves, yet there is nothing to make us question the honesty of his motivation for return given to his wives (31:3–13). He is seen as a man who has come to realize that his prosperity has been created by God. Yet this was still bound up with a real element of doubt and fear (31:31). In the moment of crisis, however, his faith shone out (31:42), and there is no reason for doubting that his words to Laban represented his real feelings. In other words Jacob was in the position of so many today; true faith and human effort and fears were strangely mixed. Even if we do not recognize this contradiction in ourselves, we meet it so often in our friends, that we should beware of condemning it too strongly in Jacob.

Laban had caught up with his son-in-law somewhere in the hills of Gilead. When they parted, Jacob moved south-wards towards the gorge of the Jabbok. This was the point of decision. Once he had reached the point where it opened out and made a way to the Jordan valley and so to Canaan, he was committed to going on or turning back. In addition, when he had brought his flocks down to the stream level, it would be very difficult to extricate them quickly, should he be attacked.

That is why, while he was resting his flocks after the forced march from Haran, Jacob sent messengers to Esau to announce his return (32:3–5). He evidently moved on down into the Jabbok valley, while he waited to hear Esau's reaction. When his returning servants came with the terrifying news that Esau was hard on their heels with four hundred men (32:6), Jacob knew himself trapped. We have grown accustomed to the large numbers in our modern civilisations and armies, that Esau's retinue of four hundred seems little out of the ordinary to us. It is modern archaeology that has brought such figures to life. It has shown us that the average population of a Canaanite town at the time was round five thousand. In the Amarna letters some centuries later we find Canaanite kings begging their Egyptian overlord for eighty, forty, or even twenty trained soldiers to help guard their cities against the barbarians that had broken into the land. So Esau's retinue could hardly mean less than dire vengeance on his brother.

In his *1984* George Orwell has as one of his central thoughts that in every person there is some concealed fear, which, if it is brought into the open, will break him down and destroy him. Whether this is, or is not, a universal fact, it is certainly very common. In Jacob it was his fear of his brother. Away in Haran Esau had seemed a long way off. In all probability God's command to Jacob to return seemed to him an implied guarantee that Esau had in some way been neutralized. Now his hurried approach at the head of his troop threw Jacob out of his stride. His first impulse was to divide all his possessions, including his wives and children, into two separated groups (32:7, 8). He knew his brother's temperament well enough to expect that his anger, hatred and injured honour would be sated and satisfied by one blood-bath, and so the other group would be spared.

This was not good enough. The plan might miscarry, and in any case the price to be paid was too heavy to be contemplated with equanimity. So we find Jacob turning to God in what may be regarded as a model prayer (32:9–12). In it he reminded God of His purpose and promises. He acknowledged his unworthiness and God's faithfulness. He concluded with a cry for help and a new reminder of God's promises.

Though he had committed all into God's hand, his heart
was not at rest. As night drew on, he chose out a princely
gift – Jesus' parable of the Good Shepherd (Matt. 18:12–14,
Lk. 15:4–7) clearly implies that in his time a flock of a
hundred sheep was a large one – which he disposed to the
best effect and sent on ahead (32:13–21). But even so he
could not sleep. In his restlessness he sent his wife and
children across the Jabbok as though to hasten the inevitable
confrontation; he waited alone for what might ensue. The
story simply tells us, "Jacob was left alone". Man has a
tremendous skill in using friends, work and circumstances
to come between him and his God, to avoid confrontation
with the all-revealing holiness of his Maker.

Outwardly the story that follows is one of the most
mysterious in the Bible. We are told that "a man wrestled
with him until the breaking of the day". Jacob himself
recognized that he had been wrestling with God (32:30),
while Hosea interprets it, "In his manhood he strove with
God. He strove with the angel and prevailed" (12:3, 4), so
suggesting that the man was an angel directly representing
God. This seems to be something completely alien to anything we may be called on to experience, until we remember that Jacob stood right at the beginning of God's deeper
revelation to men and that he had very little spiritual tradition behind him. When we grasp this, it is not too hard to
understand that what we have to experience within us had
to find external expression for Jacob. In varying measure
this is something that happens repeatedly to the young
believer in contrast to mature Christians, to the isolated
disciple in contrast to those in a strong Christian fellowship,
to early converts from heathendom in contrast to those in
lands where the Church is firmly established. Jacob's
experience was one that very many have had to share; only
its outward form was exceptional.

God was saying to Jacob, as they wrestled under the light
of the moon, "Do you trust me, Jacob?"

"Lord, you know I do!"

"What about Esau?"

"Lord, you know I cannot; you must get him out of the way somehow."

"No, Jacob; you must trust me for him also."

"No, Lord! That I can't."

"If you want my help and blessing, you must!"

"No, Lord, you ask too much; only get Esau out of the way, and you may ask what you will".

If there is a deeply hidden fear in any one of us, God must bring it to the light, if we are to see our profession of trust made a reality and we are really to be transformed by the power of Christ. When this challenge comes to us, it may well involve a wrestling with God fully comparable with Jacob's and which in its intensity can sometimes almost take on a physical dimension.

So it went on the livelong night until the first light of dawn began to show. It had to be now or never. Esau was at hand, and if Jacob did not trust now he never would. So the strange wrestler touched the hollow of Jacob's thigh and put his leg out of joint. "I must leave you now, for the day is breaking". But Jacob clung to him desperately; "I will not let you go, unless you bless me. You have crippled me; you have handed me over helpless to my brother's anger; now you must meet my need." Behind all Jacob's struggles lay the conviction that somehow he could yet circumvent his thick-skulled brother. If the worst came to the worst, he could take to his heels and escape, but now –! In spite of all his fears there was nothing left to him but to trust.

"What is your name?" "Jacob", the smart fellow. Again and again he must have boasted to his friends that he was well named, for none had been able to outsmart him in the long run. Now his world lay in ruins around him as he drank to the dregs of the cup of the vanity of human effort, wisdom and skill. "Your name shall no more be called Jacob but Israel (God strives), for you have striven with God and with men, and have prevailed." The name Israel could equally well mean "He who strives with God", but since it

is clearly intended to be honourable, "God strives" is obviously preferable. Yet the other is implicit in it, for there
would have been no need for God to have striven had Jacob
not resisted him. Jacob had prevailed at the cost of becoming a cripple, and he would prevail against men by yielding
to God.

This was not enough for Jacob. "Tell me, please, your
name". His subsequent explanation (32:30) why he called
the place of his wrestling Face-of-God (Peni-el), "For I have
seen God face to face, and yet my life is preserved", shows
that he knew well enough with whom he had been wrestling. It may be considered almost certain that he shared in
what was probably a universal superstition at the time –
another example may be found in Exod. 3:13 (cf. p. 91) –
that knowledge of the hidden, secret name of a god gave
some control over him and could ensure his help in time of
need. This is magic and the true God has no truck with
magic. The only way in which a man can be sure of the help
of the one true God is to come before him in utter weakness,
trust and dependence.

So, as the sun rose, Jacob went limping to meet his great
fear. Wonder of wonders, Esau fell on his neck and kissed
him (33:4). Over the letters of "and-he-kissed-him" (one
word in Hebrew) in Hebrew stands a row of dots, which
tradition explains as the marks of Esau's teeth, i.e. he did
not kiss Jacob but bit him. While we may dismiss this piece
of rabbinic fancy without further discussion, we may
accept the implied judgment on Esau's behaviour. There is
no suggestion in Scripture that his character had really
changed. The most likely suggestion is that God had spoken
to him as he had to Laban (31:29) and had warned him
against taking any violent action. We cannot really ignore
the implications of the four hundred men who followed
him.

When all is said and done, what is important is that God
had solved Jacob's pressing problem, not by leading him
away from it, but by bringing him to face it in weakness

dependent on God's strength. Tragic is the fact that the whole story lives in Jewish memory not as the indication of what God expects of his people Israel but rather as something that affects their diet. Hindquarters' meat has to be porged, i.e. have the sinew removed, which in many countries means that the orthodox Jew does not eat hindquarters' meat. The Israelites of old did not eat the sinew as a reminder how their ancestor became Israel; if this is forgotten, it becomes a mere bit of ritualism, which is not even commanded by the Law.

CHAPTER 8

JOSEPH AND HIS BROTHERS
(*Gen. 45, 50*)

One of the great dangers of allegory and even of thorough-going typology is that we do not adequately consider what a passage is telling us. Joseph has been an outstanding sufferer from this tendency. Though there is no support for the suggestion from the New Testament, he was very frequently been regarded as a type of Jesus Christ, or at the very least he has been compared favourably with him. As a result he is seldom looked at objectively enough.

The shortcomings in Jacob's family are obvious enough, yet we gain the impression of very real loyalty and even affection in it. There must, therefore, have been some adequate reason for the deep hatred shown to Joseph by his brothers. It is not questioned today that "the long robe with sleeves" (RSV) given him by Jacob was the sign that he now ranked as the official first-born. Chronicles shows little interest in the Joseph tribes, but in the genealogies in the first book it makes clear (5:1) that since Reuben had rightly forfeited his position, by his incest, there could be no complaint at the first-born of the other wife taking his place. In addition, especially in a large family, this position offered little real advantage.[1]

---

[1] In Israel an estate was divided into a number of equal portions, one more than the number of sons. The birthright of the first-born was to take two of the portions. Obviously with twelve sons the extra thirteenth would not arouse much envy. At the time the extra tribal portion for Joseph could not have been foreseen.

The clue seems to be offered by Jacob's reaction to Joseph's second dream (37:10). Since a significant dream was regarded as coming from outside the dreamer, it would have been unfair to rebuke Joseph for having it. The reason must have been the air of self-satisfaction with which he told it. With this in mind we are probably justified in seeing him flaunting his first-born's garment in front of his brothers, especially Reuben. In addition it is probable that we are to place an unfavourable interpretation on the statement that he brought a bad report of the sons of Bilhah and Zilpah to Jacob (37:2). By the time he was seventeen (37:2), unwise favouritism had gone far to making Joseph a very unpleasant young man. But such are the results of typological exposition that to say this in public may lead to bitter opposition. As I see him gagged, bound and thrown over the back of a camel like a sack of potatoes by the Midianite traders, I can picture him remembering his dreams and contemplating the revenge he would enjoy wreaking on his brothers in days to come.

It is rare for the Bible to indicate explicitly how the Spirit works in the transformation of character. We are next shown Joseph, not as a typical slave giving the mimimum of grudging service, but working so whole-heartedly that he caught Potiphar's attention, and so was brought into his house from his labour out of doors (39:2). "And he was in the house of his master" (AV, RSV), "He lived in the house of his Egyptian master (NEB, TEV), and "He lodged in the house of his Egyptian master" (JB) all ignore the Hebrew idiom, which clearly indicates a further step in the improvement of his fortunes. Possibly Joseph recognized that he was reaping what he had sown, and so accepted God's judgment on him.

We next find him in charge of his master's house (39:4). No slave could hold such a position without being able to read and write. It is impossible to establish whether Joseph as favourite son would have learnt these skills while he was still at home. In itself it is quite probable, but if he had, it

would, if the Amarna letters of a somewhat later date are
any guide, have been in cuneiform, not in Egyptian hiero-
glyphics, which were notoriously difficult to master. His
ability to do so implies that Joseph was able to win the
confidence and favour of the head-slave at the time, and also
that he must have taken advantage of every spare moment
granted him. God helped Joseph to reach the top, but Joseph
helped God to help him.

The second stage in Joseph's spiritual education was his
learning that confidence in man was vain. From 40:3 we
learn that the prison in which Joseph found himself was
under the control of the captain of the guard, i.e. Potiphar.
His subordinate, the keeper of the prison, would not have
dared to show Joseph favour (39:21–23) without Potiphar's
permission, for it was on a charge of mortally offending his
master that Joseph had been thrown into jail. This view of
things is confirmed by the fact that Potiphar himself made
him attendant on two important state prisoners (40:4). The
titles chief butler and chief baker conceal from us the fact
that they were important court officials, who were obviously under suspicion of having been involved in some
intrigue against the Pharaoh. In other words, Joseph was
forced to realise that in spite of his loyal and whole-hearted
service, his master, knowing full well that his wife's accusa-
tion was baseless, had callously sacrificed him for the sake of
matrimonial peace.

His second disappointment was probably greater.
Pharaoh's chief butler failed to tell his master about Joseph,
when he was restored to office, though he had nothing to
lose by doing so. "Nothing to lose" – that was the point.
When he saw Pharaoh, a god incarnate, desperate to discover what the warning from the gods conveyed in dream-
form might mean, he knew that a revived memory would
almost certainly bring its reward, and so he remembered
Joseph (41:9–13).

Through his double disappointment Joseph had learnt
not merely not to put his trust in man, but also not to trust in

himself, two things which very often do not go together.
With all the resources of Egypt at his disposal it would have
been child's play for him to discover all about his family, the
more so as Canaan was clearly under Egyptian control at the
time (50:4–14). He knew, however, that once he knew for
certain, he might not be able to resist the urge to see his
father and Benjamin again. He also knew his father well
enough to know that a premature disclosure of what had
happened might so arouse his anger as to scatter his family
for ever. So he was prepared to wait until God should fulfil
his word. This was the easier for him because his later
experience confirmed that he could rely on his earlier
dreams, which would surely come to pass at the time of
God's choosing.

The seven prosperous years came and went according to
God's word, and with them a wife and two sons followed to
ease the ache of an empty heart. Then followed the years of
famine. When Joseph heard that it had extended to Canaan
(42:5), he sensed that the time for his brothers' coming
could not be far distant. The idea that Joseph made himself
personally responsible for the selling of the grain is, of
course, ludicrous, though we may be certain that he made
frequent, unannounced visits to the selling centres. He will
have been as conscientious in his prosperity as he had been
in the bitter years of adversity. But no foreigners could
enter Egypt without permission, and Joseph will have given
instructions to the frontier posts to let him know with all
speed, if a group of Hebrews should ask permission to come
and buy.

A year and more passed (45:6), and at last his brothers,
arrived but without Benjamin. When they arrived at the
selling centre to which they had been directed they dis-
covered that the Chief Minister was there on a tour of
inspection, and before him they were brought. They scarce
ventured to lift their eyes to his glory, while he spoke to
them through an interpreter.

Joseph sifted his brothers mercilessly and found that the

years had changed them. They were conscious of their sin against him and they were prepared to sacrifice themselves for their father and Benjamin. Their abject prostration before him was in itself a sign that God's dream-given promise was coming true.

Joseph's intense emotion and tears (42:24; 45:1, 2) show that he had long since forgiven his brothers. Indeed, it is clear that we do not have the right to speak of forgiveness in this context, though there has to be forgiveness by God. He did not, as we so often do, when we are called on to forgive, brush away or make little of what had been done. Twice directly, once indirectly (45:4, 5, 8) he stressed what they had done. Then he balanced this by insisting three times that God had been behind it all (45:5, 7, 8).

So often we base ourselves on the New Testament and say that "in everything God works for good with those who love him" (Rom. 8:28). Yet we speak glibly of forgiving those who have been God's instruments for the working out of his gracious purposes for our good. We may even speak of the difficulty of forgiving, as though it were necessary to forgive our benefactors.

It is no unusual experience for many to find that the even tenor of their life has been interrupted and violently changed by the thoughtlessness, brutality, selfishness, or even malice of others, only to discover that the new path they then followed was obviously the one of God's choice. Why should we blame the instruments, when the main fault lay in our insensibility to God's will and guidance, which forced him to use instruments like these? Joseph was not granted the knowledge why Israel had to go down to Egypt, but he knew full well that it was not simply to escape famine. The God who had brought both plenty and need at the time of his choosing could have dispensed with the latter. Just like his being sold into slavery, it was a means to an end beyond his knowledge.

We seldom realise how often and with what skill God uses the wrath of man to work out his purposes. Though in his wisdom he had to bring his people into Egypt, he placed them in Goshen under conditions where they could increase and prosper, and yet be relatively untouched by Egyptian thought and idolatry. This could be accomplished only by there being his agent in the seat of power, and this man was Joseph. Even had Jacob been willing to let his son go down to Egypt, he could hardly have achieved the position of second man in the kingdom, the more so as he was a foreigner. They had to ask pardon of God, these brothers of his who had been so heartless, but there was nothing for him to forgive.

Seventeen years passed (47:28), and Jacob's turn came to join Abraham and Isaac in the family burial-place in the cave of Machpelah. Once the days of mourning and the funeral were over the brothers appeared humbly before Joseph (50:16, 18 NEB – in the former verse NEB follows LXX) and told him that their father had given them a last command, that they should ask Joseph's forgiveness for all the wrong they had done to him, and now in fear and trembling they made this their humble petition. To Joseph's tears they added their own (50:18 NEB, with the change of one letter in Hebrew); they added, "You see, we are your slaves" (NEB), which was equivalent to saying that Joseph had the right and power to do what he liked with them.

Theirs were tears of fear, but Joseph wept from a well-nigh broken heart. It is not likely that he paid much attention to the alleged message from his dead father. Though it is not inconsistent with what we know of him, he would have been able and willing to say it personally to Joseph, when he made arrangements for his funeral (47:29–31). It is likely that his brothers were availing themselves of the convenient fact that the dead do not rise up to call us liars. But his brothers' words and actions showed that for the best part of twenty years they had not believed him and had thought that he was only biding his time for vengeance for his father's sake. Now as official first-born and the power behind the throne of Egypt he could do as he liked.

Joseph in his answer stressed that sin cannot be made less by vagueness of language: "You meant evil against me". In the long run we never do any good by finding excuses, by minimizing wrong, by calling black grey. But he asked the question that all who are wronged should ask: "Am I in the place of God?"

The principle behind it has been grasped by British law. Neither the person who claims to have been wronged nor his kith and kin determine the issue. At least in serious cases it is left to a jury of ordinary men and women to decide whether in fact wrong has been done. If they say yes, the penalty, if any, is fixed not by them but by the judge, who in most cases knows far more about the accused than did the jury, when they gave their verdict. This is an analogy of a position we very often find ourselves in. We cannot avoid having to decide from time to time whether an action was right or wrong. If we have suffered from it, it is generally wise to leave the decision to others, for it may be hard for us to see how much blame we bear. In every case, however, we must never forget that it is God who is the judge, and that he alone is competent to apportion the blame and to fix whatever penalties there may be.

So in asking, "Am I in the place of God?" Joseph was telling his brothers that peace for a guilty conscience and forgiveness for evil done had to be sought in God's presence, not in man's. That did not mean that where it was possible reparation should not be done. That is a principle that is clearly laid down in the Law. While not only the sin-offering but also the guilt-offering were brought to God, and in the antitype have been brought by Jesus Christ, yet reparation had to be made to the one wronged.

Yet what reparation could they make? Joseph had all a man could desire and far more than he would ever have had, if they had not sinned against him. In addition he could say out of a full heart, "God meant it for good". The one thing he wanted from them was that they should believe him.

He had learnt in the school of suffering what a privilege it was to be allowed to suffer for God, so that God's purpose might be fulfilled. We can hardly suggest that he knew that ultimately the chief sufferer would be God himself. There are increasing intimations of this in the growing revelation of God in the Old Testament, but we can hardly look for the knowledge in Genesis. Where this realisation dawns on the sufferer, the desire for vengeance and reparation disappear. There may be deep sorrow for those that have done wrong and a longing for the restoration. In some measure the prayer will go up, "Father, forgive them, for they do not know what they are doing".

This prayer of our Lord's as he was nailed to the cross sums up what has been said of Joseph. There is here the recognition that men, whether we call them good or bad, do not grasp the role they are playing in the onward march of events. There is the acknowledgement of the fact of evil and of the need of forgiveness. But Jesus, suffering as the perfect man, does not forgive them, for he has nothing to forgive – they have simply been blindly working out God's purposes for the redemption of mankind. So he entrusts them to the mercy of the all-merciful God, who was in Christ reconciling the world to himself.

It is perhaps a sign of true and genuine reconciliation that when Joseph came to die at the age of a hundred and ten, it was not to his sons and grandsons that he gave commandment about his body that would be embalmed but to his brothers, or at least to those who were still alive. By this he showed that he knew that he could have complete confidence in them and their descendants.

CHAPTER 9

THE BURNING BUSH
(*Exod. 3*)

Jacob died in Egypt, and one by one his sons followed him. By the fourth generation there had been a change of dynasty in Egypt.[1] With the coming to power of new rulers much in the past was forgotten or studiously ignored. The growing clan of Hebrews in Goshen near the eastern frontier was regarded as a menace, should the unruly tribes of Syria and Canaan seek to break into the Nile Delta, as had the Hyksos centuries earlier. The Egyptians sought to tame the freedom-loving semi-nomads and reduce their numbers by drafting them into the forced-labour system of Egypt, which provided for the building and upkeep of the country's temples, tombs and palaces. When this failed, more drastic methods were tried to reduce their number.

It seems clear that the effort to kill the Hebrew boys at birth did not last very long. The attitude of Pharaoh's daughter shows that there were those who regarded government policy as inhumane, and they were doubtless soon able to change it or make it inoperative. It did result, however, in a Hebrew once more finding himself in the seats of the mighty.

It is customary to stress all that Moses will have gained by his education and position, cf. Acts 7:22, though we should

---

[1] Cf. Gen. 15:13–16, Exod. 6:16–18, 20; 22:40. For a discussion of the apparent contradiction here, cf. NBD, "Chronology of the Old Testament".

do well to regard with the greatest suspicion the tradition quoted by Josephus (*Ant. II x.* 2) that he gained a great victory over the Ethiopians and married the daughter of their king. The whole colouring of the story suggests a fertile imagination. The Bible, in any case, ignores this aspect of his life and does not even suggest a motive for his interventions in favour of his compatriots. The statement that the Pharaoh sought to kill Moses (Exod. 2:15) suggests that rightly or wrongly he suspected that Moses was plotting against him.

We may take it that the three periods of forty years into which Moses' life falls are round figures, but they do stress that all the years of education, civilization and culture were balanced by an equal period of labour and semi-barbarism. Among relics of the past from Egypt there has survived the story of Sinuhe, an Egyptian noble, who in fear of having incurred the Pharaoh's anger fled to a semi-nomadic tribe in Canaan or southern Syria. The story brings out how, in spite of honour and prosperity, and a marriage blessed with children, he regarded permission to return to Egypt to spend an honourable old age there as the crowning mercy. It is difficult for us to grasp the contrast between the palaces of Egypt's capital and the tents of the priest of Midian.

For our purpose it is of minimum importance who the Pharaoh from whom Moses fled may have been, which area was claimed by the Midianites in the time of Moses, or where Horeb-Sinai lay – the site of "the mountain of God" (Exod. 3:1) is far from certain. Somewhere in that wild, desert land Moses was pasturing his father-in-law's sheep. He had sunk to the level of his ancestor Jacob, "a wandering Aramean" (Deut. 26:5), before God had begun to make him prosper. Suddenly he saw a desert thorn-bush burst into flame, something not uncommon in that intense heat. But instead of being burnt up in a few minutes, this one continued to burn with a steady flame. Moses' curiosity, perhaps a relic of his Egyptian education, stirred within him, and he went over to see what was happening.

Jesus' invitation, "Come to me, all who labour and are heavy laden" (Matt. 11:28), has a far deeper and wider meaning than those who think purely of the burden of sin realise. It is a moot point whether riches or the crushing burden of daily toil numb the soul and make it insensible to God's voice the more quickly and surely. The hard toil of the nomadic shepherd had not dulled Moses' senses so completely that he had no longer eyes for anything outside the daily round.

As he looked at the flame burning steadily in the bush, a voice sounded in his ears, "Take off your sandals; you are standing on holy ground" – holy because God was there. Moses, awe-struck, obeyed, and the voice went on, "I am your father's God, the God of Abraham, the God of Isaac and the God of Jacob". In holy awe Moses covered his face, for now he knew that the flame marked the presence of God.

Traditional Jewish exegesis understands "your father's God" as a collective, i.e., the God of your fathers, and this is the reading of the Samaritan Pentateuch; it is also the usual Christian understanding. We may, however, question it. A collective in such a setting is improbable and probably without any real parallel. We should rather understand that before Moses had to leave his parents' home in order to be known as the son of Pharaoh's daughter, Amram had seen to it that he understood the faith that had encouraged him and his mother to shelter their baby, and that it was this faith that accounted for the existence of his people.

It has been usual to look on the bush as symbolic, and it may be so. It could be a picture of Moses, dried up and fruitless after half a life-time in exile, yet capable of so receiving the Spirit of God, that he would become probably the greatest of the Old Testament prophets (Deut. 34:10). Equally it could depict Israel, enslaved, fearful, corrupt, in whose midst, however, God would live down the centuries, until he became incarnate in a Jewish maiden, and indeed until he had worked out his purpose in the people of

his choice. So, too, we may use it of the Church with all its
imperfections and failures, but yet bearing the light and
power of the Messiah to the uttermost parts of the earth. For
our story, however, it is merely the means by which God
can test whether Moses would still respond to the super-
natural, or whether the hardships of desert life had so brutal-
ised him that he could not think of more than mere subsis-
tence.

The voice went on to tell him that the time had come for
the promises to the patriarchs to be fulfilled, and that he was
to be God's messenger to the Pharaoh, that he might lead
the people out of Egypt. Here at last we see the real reason
for the forty years at the Pharaoh's court. The sequel is
comprehensible only when we remember that no commoner, especially if he were a foreigner, could have
demanded admission to the Pharaoh's presence. Moses was
still officially a member of the royal family with all the
privileges that implied.

Moses' answer betrayed how the iron of the long, empty
years had entered his soul: "Who am I that I should go?" To
that there was no answer, and indeed no answer possible,
for he was, after all, the tinder-dry, barren desert-bush, but
there was the promise, "I will be with you". Then there was
the sign: when all had been accomplished, the people
brought out of the house of bondage would worship God
on that very mountain. Such is the essential principle of
faith. However much God may condescend to the weakness
and doubts of his children, ultimately obedience to God's
call and guidance involves a faith that is prepared to wait for
its confirmation instead of having an immediate sign. To
demand more than that is to walk by sight, not by faith. The
children of Israel were given miraculous signs, but these did
not free them of doubt.

Moses answered the challenge to his faith by questioning
Israel's faith. They might, he said, ask for God's name.
What was he to answer? The more we consider this appar-
ently innocent question, the more our suspicions should be

aroused. Some forty years after, so far as we can tell, losing
the last vestiges of touch with his people, it is improbable
that Moses would have any real idea of how they would
receive God's message. In any case they knew, just as well as
Moses, that the name Yahweh – cf. footnote on p. 20 – was
the name used by the God of the Patriarchs, and had Moses
given them any other, they would have suspected him of
being a fraud. As A. B. Davidson said in HDB (Vol. II, p.
200), "A new name would have been in those days a new
God". Exod. 6:20 shows that already through his mother's
name, Jochebed, Moses was familiar with the divine name.

The thought is almost irresistible that behind Moses'
question lay a deep-rooted heathen superstition. It is, of
course, true that as M. Noth says, "In ancient Eastern
thought the name of the person who existed was a necessary
part of his existence and one knew of a reality only if one
was able to pronounce its 'name'. In the same way Moses
will only be able to make the Israelites believe in the reality
of his encounter with God if he is able to tell them the name
of the God who appeared to him" (*Exodus*, p. 42). But once
this God is linked with the God of the patriarchs, whose
name was known, there must be something deeper.

The idea was that in addition to the many titles given to a
deity he had a secret name known only to the initiated, and
that to call on him by that name gave the worshipper some
control over the deity he worshipped, (cf. p. 77). Moses'
thought probably was that if he was to go on God's errand,
he might as well guarantee that he could make certain of
God's aid. Should anyone consider this derogatory to
Moses, he should bear in mind that there is no suggestion
that the forty years in Midian had been a time of deepening
knowledge of and fellowship with God, and the whole
story of God's meeting with him at the bush hardly suggests
that he was then the man of deep faith he later showed
himself to be.

Instead of answering Moses' request, God explained
what his name Yahweh meant – this seems to be the force

of Exod. 6:2, 3, i.e., not that the name was unknown, but that its meaning and implications were. There are many suggestions how and why this was, but since none are provable, and the subject is irrelevant to our purpose, they are best left unmentioned. God explained the force of Yahweh by linking it with the verb *hayah*, to be or to become. How the enigmatic *'ehyeh 'asher 'ehyeh* is to be translated is a matter of controversy, and nothing would be gained by listing the dozens of suggestions that have been made. In fact the main translations of the Old Testament into English in text or margin opt for two chief variations.

(a) "I am who (that or what) I am" – NEB "I am; that is who I am" means essentially the same. Some few have interpreted this purely as a rebuke to Moses. He had no business to pry into that which God had not yet revealed. He must bow to the fact of God and accept him in the measure he had made himself known. There can be little doubt that this element cannot be completely eliminated from God's reply, however we interpret it, but it cannot be its chief purpose, even though Moses merited a rebuke of this kind.

The usual understanding is that God is here stressing his essential unchangeableness, his separation from everything that could make him in any way dependent on his creation. This is, of course true, and one could quote numerous passages of Scripture to establish it. It seems too to have been the way in which LXX understood it. This is natural, for Alexandrian Jewry had been influenced by Greek thought in which the static, unchanging nature of deity had been stressed. It also fitted the outlook of Maimonides (1135–1204), who was strongly under the influence of Aristotle.

Quite apart, however, from the question whether this interpretation really suits the context, it is doubtful whether the basic meaning of *hayah*, which seldom means mere existence, and above all the use of the imperfect tense used, justify it. A. B. Davidson could write in *The Theology of the*

Old Testament, "I do not think there is in the Hebrew Bible a case of the imperfect of this verb having the sense of the English *present*" (p. 55). So we come to the second interpretation.

(b) In the margin of RV, RSV, NEB, TEV we find the rendering "I will be what I will be". Yahweh is the God who reveals himself and enters into covenant relationship with his people. Nothing will invalidate that revelation or relationship. Even when that revelation reached its fulness in the Son, the eternal Word, there is need of the Holy Spirit to lead into all truth. Even though the record of revelation is closed, John Robinson was indubitably correct, when he said in his farewell address to those of his congregation leaving Delft Haven in the *Speedwell* for the New World, "I am verily persuaded the Lord hath more truth yet to break forth out of His holy word" (1620). Knowledge of God is essential to salvation (Jn. 17:3), but only when we see face to face, shall we understand fully as we have been fully understood (1 Cor. 13:12, 13). So God was telling Moses that in faith he had to go forward on the basis of what he knew of him, and in so doing he would learn more of God, and the new would be a deepening of what was already known. In addition he would discover that the God who called and sent would also accompany. Similarly although Jesus is the same, yesterday, to-day and for ever, none but a man who has lost his way will claim that he has come to a full knowledge of him.

It is worth mentioning that when the name Yahweh appears in a compounded proper name, it is always in a shortened form, either Ye- or Yo- (English Je- or Jo-), e.g. Jehoahaz, Jehoram, Jonathan, Josiah, Jochebed, or -iah, e.g, Ahaziah, Zedekiah. This can adequately be explained only by assuming that these forms are derived from Yah, English Jah. It can well be that this was the original form of the title, and that now God added H to it – cf. Abram, Abrahm, p. 52 – so linking it with *hayah* and giving it a fuller meaning than it had earlier possessed.

God went on by implication to rebuke Moses' suggestion of lack of belief on the part of Israel. They would believe (3:18); the difficulty would come from the Pharaoh, but this would turn out to Israel's gain. Moses continued to hide his lack of trust by suggesting unwillingness to believe on the part of Israel (4:1). So God gave him three signs, which would, if necessary, convince the people (4:2–9). They did prove effective in creating trust (4:29–31), but it might well have been that the elders of Israel would have believed in any case, even as God had foretold. It could be that they would have shown more faith later, had Moses not faced them with signs from the first.

Moses showed his real state of heart by pleading that he was slow and hesitant of speech (4:10, NEB). Even had it been true, it was an insult to God, who had chosen and called him. The God who gave him power to do miracles could look after his mouth and indeed after all his faculties (4:11). Apart from Moses' plea here there is, however, no suggestion anywhere that Moses had any difficulty in speaking. True, in Midian he had had little opportunity for oratory, and he may well have felt that his Egyptian had become rusty. No, it is clear evidence of unwillingness and lack of faith. Obviously, some of the rabbis, for whom criticism of Moses was near to blasphemy, invented a legend to explain how he as a child, when in danger of death, had had his lips badly burnt, and this permanently impaired his speech!

Moses' answer was "O Lord, send, I pray thee, by the hand of him whom Thou wilt send" (4:13, RV), which Rashi's grandson Rashbam (12th century) rightly interpreted as "send by anyone but myself". The answer was the more impertinent, because by calling Yahweh "Lord" he acknowledged his right to send him. No wonder that God was angry. It could be that God would have used Aaron as Moses' mouthpiece in any case, for it was usual at the time for the great and mighty to communicate their will through a spokesman, and the use of Aaron will have enhanced

Moses' stature in the eyes of the Pharaoh. But the position enhanced Aaron's stature in the eyes of Israel, and this involved Moses in personal trouble (Num. 12:1) and, it may be, made the sin of the golden bull the more readily possible (Exod. 32:1). It may also explain why Moses had to pass on the priesthood to his brother, though he had acted as the priest at the making of the covenant and the consecration of the Tabernacle and of Aaron and his sons.

Let us not end on this note. We may take comfort from the fact that once Moses bowed to God's will, God was able to use him as the prime instrument in the forging of Israel into a nation and the establishing of a Law which stood unparalleled until its divine giver took on himself the likeness of sinful flesh and appeared as the heir of David's line.

CHAPTER 10

THE CROSSING OF THE RED SEA
(*Exod. 14*)

On the third evening after they had hurriedly left their
homes in Egypt the people of Israel found their way barred
by the waters of the Sea of Reeds, a name normally, but
questionably, rendered as the Red Sea. With a shock they
realized that they had yet to cross the Egyptian frontier. To
the tired people came the command to pitch their tents for
the night. Scarcely had they done so, when a cloud of dust
was seen on the horizon. It drew nearer, and soon the sound
of horses, of chariots and of soldiers' shouts was heard,
while at times the dust cloud was broken by the glint of the
setting sun on armour and weapons. A shout of dismay and
terror rose from the Israelites, for they realised that
Pharaoh's chariotry was on their heels. Servitude in Egypt
would have been better than death in the wilderness.

Suddenly the sight of their pursuers was blotted out. The
strange pillar of cloud that had led them from Rameses
through Succoth and Etham had now moved between them
and their pursuers, bewildering them and preventing them
from moving forward. As darkness fell, its fiery heart
glowed red, assuring them of God's watchful eye and protection.

With the onset of night a hot, strong, east wind began to
blow. The people sheltered as they could from the driving
sand. Then the light of the moon, only a few days past full,
was blotted out by thick clouds, and a violent thunder-

storm broke over Israelites and Egyptians alike (Psa. 77:18). Then the ground heaved and shook in earthquake shock (Pss. 77:18; 114:4, 6). There has been a surprising ignoring by many of the poetic accounts of Israel's experiences at the Sea of Reeds.

The clouds cleared and under the bright light of the moon Israel saw a clear pathway of dry land before them, though to right and left the waters of the Sea of Reeds could be seen. The story attributes this to the force of the wind (14:21), but it may well be that in addition the earthquake had temporarily lifted a strip of the sea-bed as well.

The command went round the people to be ready to march. Whether under other circumstances Israel would have dared to tread this strange path, it is hard to say. Fear of death, however, drives men to risk what they would otherwise never think of doing, and so they moved steadily forward where man had never stood before. As the Egyptian troops realized what was happening they followed. It would seem clear from archaeological evidence that while the Pharaoh sent his chariots after the Israelites, he preferred to remain on dry land himself.

Even when the Egyptians sensed that the Israelites were moving, the pillar of cloud prevented them from seeing what was happening. To right and left they could see the waters of the Sea of Reeds glittering in the moonlight. They were in real fact a protective wall, preventing any attempt to outflank the fleeing people. It was only as the pillar of cloud glowing with fire started passing along the strip of dry land to act as Israel's rearguard that the position became clear. Because of this delay the Egyptian chariots had advanced no more than half way by the time the last Israelite stood safely on the other side.

Suddenly a strange unease and panic seized the pursuers. The narrative explains it simply by saying "the Lord in the pillar of cloud and of fire looked down on the host of the Egyptians, and discomfitted the host of the Egyptians". At the same time the chariot wheels began to be embedded in the sand. If the suggestion made earlier is correct, the sea bed was returning to its normal level, as so often happens after an earthquake, and so the first signs of returning water became apparent.

As Moses stood under the first signs of dawn on the eastern shore of the Sea of Reeds, God commanded him to stretch out his hand, presumably holding his rod, cf. verse 16, over the sea, so that its waters might return. Probably only one who has barely been saved at the last moment from drowning can even begin to imagine the horror of what followed. As the panic-stricken Egyptians turned to flee, throwing aside armour and weapons, they suddenly realized that they were in rapidly rising water. This lasted only a moment and then a veritable tidal wave swept over them. For a few there will have been a despairing effort to swim to safety; most, however, will have been entangled among the madly plunging, screaming horses still attached to the chariots. It may be that something of the horror of it lies behind the Talmudic passage, where R. Johanan expressed the view that God does not rejoice in the downfall of the wicked. "The ministering angels wanted to sing a hymn at the destruction of the Egyptians, but God said: "My children lie drowned in the sea, and will you sing?"

We need not be surprised that we find Israel, led by Moses, singing a song of glad triumph in praise to God, while Miriam led the women in the refrain: "I will sing to the Lord, for he has triumphed gloriously; horse and rider he has thrown into the sea." The rider was not a cavalry man, for he did not exist at the time in the Fertile Crescent, but the rider in the chariot. The leading thought of this song of praise is "triumphed gloriously", which means much more than that God had destroyed the Egyptian chariot force and set his people free.

There is a perplexing element in the story of the plagues that God brought on Egypt, which is often overlooked. It is often assumed that they were the means used by God to make the Pharaoh bow to his will and let his people go.

True enough, when God first sent Moses back to Egypt, he told him, "I know well that the king of Egypt will not give you leave unless he is compelled" (Exod. 3:19, NEB). But before Moses returned, God said to him, "I will harden his heart, so that he will not let the people go" (4:21), and in the following story there is far more stress on God's act of hardening than on the Pharaoh's hardening of his own heart.

There is only one adequate answer to this problem. We are told, "Pharaoh will not listen to you, so I will assert my power in Egypt, and with mighty acts of judgment I will bring my people, the Israelites, out of Egypt ... then Egypt will know that I am the Lord" (7:4, 5 NEB). This knowledge comes through God's mighty acts, which teach his nature and his power. They may be experienced in blessing as does Israel in 6:7, or in judgment. In other words the plagues were not simply a way of breaking down the Egyptians' obstinacy; they were a means of revelation to Israel and Egypt alike. More than that; they were specially chosen, for "on all the gods of Egypt I will execute judgments" (12:12).

It is now generally agreed that the first nine plagues were intensifications of natural phenomena which plague Egypt to this day. The gods of Egypt were all nature gods in one form or another, so Jehovah's power over nature was in itself a demonstration of the powerlessness of the corresponding Egyptian deities. In certain cases definite gods were involved, and if we knew more of Egyptian religion, we might discover that this was so in all cases. The first affected the Nile (7:14–21), which was one of the greatest of the Egyptian deities. The frog (8:1–7) was linked with the gods Hapi and Heqt. Various kinds of cattle (9:1–7) were sacred to a variety of deities, and the darkening of the sun (10:21–23), presumably by a terrible sand-storm, was a blow delivered at the worship of the sun, Egypt's chief god. The tenth plague, its indubitably miraculous nature, being shown by death smiting all the first born, and them only, showed Jehovah's lordship over life and death, which were Egyptian religion's greatest preoccupation. In this way simultaneously Israel learnt the absolute supremacy of Jehovah over any and every force in nature, and Egypt was shown the folly of its religion.

Egypt was supremely the land where the regularities of nature were evident. As a result it was the first civilization to discover the true solar calendar. Indeed, for most of its citizens the round of human life was foreseeable and would be upset only by disease or accident. Man was little more than an expression of nature, and so in the Egyptian pantheon the distinction between gods, men and animals largely vanished. The Pharaoh could be regarded as a god, the result of a god's visit to his mother's bed, and animals could be regarded as divinities, many of the gods being represented in semi-animal shape. Moses stressed that God's love and care were far more important than all uniformities that nature might offer. In Deut. 11:10–12 he praised the promised land, not because, like Egypt, it was completely under man's control, but because it was dependent on God for its rain. "The eyes of the Lord your God are always upon it, from the beginning of the year to the end of the year".

Man's apparent control of nature ultimately makes him a slave of nature; it is only in his dependence upon God that man reaches his true stature. We see the same today, where the more the man uses the resources of his scientific knowledge, the more he becomes enslaved by it. It is only, when he allows his studies and knowledge to show him how infinitely greater God, the Creator, is that he learns true freedom.

There is probably a dark side to every developed nature religion known to us. Disaster strikes man at the least expected moments. Sometimes it can be explained by rivalry between different deities, sometimes one finds the solution in some offence, deliberate or accidental, offered to a deity – a well-known example of this will be found in the opening of Homer's Iliad. There is, however, always the haunting fear that it may be due to a break-down of the power of the gods, that there are dark forces that threaten the very existence of order.

For the Israelites, brought up in the thought-world of the Ancient Near-East, these dark forces were symbolized by the waters of the sea. In the mythologies that surrounded them the ordered world of nature had sprung from the victory of the gods of order over the powers of chaos, but it was believed that they were still capable of breaking out again in a new life and death struggle. Man's religion was, at least from one point of view, regarded as his throwing his whole weight on the side of the gods of order.

Especially in the myths of Canaan, chaos was personified by the sea, the ruler of which was the seven-headed Lothan or Leviathan. It is easy enough to grasp the reason for this. The Mediterranean, being an enclosed sea, shows very little of the ordered ebb and flow of the tides, which speak of a higher power in control of it. Men saw in it rather the chaotic powers of evil, cf. Isa. 57:20, uncontrolled and uncontrollable.

These concepts were taken over at least by Israel's poetry and transformed. Asaph saw God crushing the many heads of Leviathan (Psa. 74:14, where the reference is both to creation and to the crossing of the Red Sea), while Psa. 104:26 looks on Leviathan as no more than God's prize aquarium exhibit. In the same psalm (verses 6–9) the taming of the sea and the fixing of its bounds are stressed as a major factor in creation.

We find a variation in the thought in Psa. 29. The poem itself obviously springs out of a tremendous and devastating storm that swept through the country from North to South, breaking and uprooting cedars and oaks. For some the roar of the tempest may have presaged the breaking-in of chaos but the psalmist heard only the voice of God, re-echoed in the heavenly temple by the angelic cry of *Glory*. It is most probable that the storm-wind brought torrential rain and flooding with it and so revived memories

of the most dreadful incident in man's past, Noah's flood. It
may very well be that ancient Near-Eastern fears of a possible resurgence of chaos were mainly based on the horrors
of Noah's flood. The Gilgamesh Epic describes the terror of
the gods during the flood as follows, "Even the gods were
afraid at the deluge, took to flight and went up to heaven of
Anu, cowered they like dogs and crouched down at the
outer defences", but the Psalmist calmly states:

> Jehovah sat as king at the Flood;
> Yea, Jehovah sitteth as king for ever (29:10, RV),

thus reaffirming God's promise in Gen. 8:22. All that happens in nature and in human government is under the
control of God's rule. The renderings of RSV, NEB, TEV
ignore the fact that the word used, *mabul*, is found only in
contexts involving Noah's flood.

All this helps to explain why God led Israel through the
sea and overwhelmed the Egyptian forces in it. It is relatively easy, far easier than many imagine, to put one's trust
in God and not in man, when one finds oneself amid the
regularities of human life, where the future seems reasonably forseeable, and the welfare state and insurance policies
seem to cushion oneself, wife and family, against the ruder
winds and misfortunes of life. When, however, all standards and landmarks seem to vanish and accepted norms of
behaviour are no more, to go forward in faith can be very
difficult – apart from the fact that it is often the only way
open – especially when one has no defence against the
violence and anarchy one is likely to meet. This is particularly the case when, as in the case of Job, it is recognized,
accepted, traditional, spiritual landmarks that have been
swept away.

The Egyptians had to perish, not as a punishment, for one
can hardly maintain that the country's chariot corps was in
any special way responsible for the treatment of Israel, but
to underline that the forces which God had unleashed were a

real peril. Israel, however, now knew, or should have
known, that even in the desert (another recognized picture
of chaos) the God who led them was in complete control of
the hostile environment.

It is worth reminding ourselves that this note is struck
elsewhere in the Old Testament. For a variety of reasons
Jonah was not prepared to face the might of Nineveh with
the message God had entrusted to him, until he experienced
God's protecting and chastening hand in the great waters
and the fish's belly – though it was not Leviathan, it must
have seemed so to the runaway prophet. Jeremiah, before
he could bring God's message of judgment in all its fulness
to Jerusalem, had to see the earth reduced to its primeval
chaos, as God spoke in wrath (4:23–26). Isaiah could
appreciate the miracle of transformation involved in the
resurrection of the dead (25:6–9; 26:19) only as he first saw
returning chaos used by God as his instrument of judgment
(ch. 24). This is, of course, one of the main messages of
Revelation and is implicit in the biblical teaching of the Day
of the Lord and the Return of Christ.

CHAPTER 11

THE MOUNT OF THE LAW
(Exod. 19, 20)

Qohelet tells us that God "has put eternity into man's mind" (Eccles. 3:11), and because of that, man seeks the fixed and permanent amid all the flux and change of life. He turns both physically and in memory to the places that have played a decisive part in his life. Even more, if he is a religious man, he will seek the holy sites of his religion and his personal experience. Though it takes a less obvious form, this is as true of Protestant movements as of traditionalist ones.

To a great extent God delivered Israel from its seeking after holy places by exalting Mt Zion and its temple to a pre-eminence that reduced the other places that had played their part in the nation's spiritual history to little more than historical sites. If this is not always true of more unsophisticated Judaism today, it is mainly due to the corrupting influence of popular Christianity and Islam. So few Christians have been able to grasp the liberating power of the knowledge of Christ's abiding presence in every place and situation.

One result of this tendency to ignore holy places was that the time came when Israel completely forgot the situation of Sinai-Horeb, the mount of the Law. Our present identifications are the result of monkish speculation in the fourth century and have as doubtful validity as most of the "holy sites" pointed out to credulous pilgrims. The rabbis wisely said that the Torah was given in the desert, so that no nation could make a special claim to it. In the same way God has seen to it that we cannot go to any one spot in the desert and affirm with certainty that it was here that God revealed his character and will to Israel and through Israel to mankind.

As the pillar of cloud and fire led Israel to the mountain, Moses' heart must have leapt within him, for he recognized that here God had spoken to him in the burning bush and was now on the point of fulfilling the sign he had then given him (Exod. 3:12). Though no more than a year had elapsed, the spot where the bush had been was doubtless no longer identifiable, but the mountain was there, and the people had been brought to it to serve God, even as he had promised.

The people pitched their tents and waited, wondering what would happen next. Suddenly they saw Moses beginning to climb the mountain. Was he going to tell God, "I have accomplished the task thou didst give me to do; here is thy people"? Then, not from a flame of fire in a desert bush, but out of the very heart of the mountain came the voice of God. If the dried up bush had spoken of Israel's need and Moses' weakness, so now the bare and arid rocks of Sinai testified to the people's heart of stone, over which Jehovah would yet triumph. The voice gave Moses a message for the people.

"If you will obey my voice and keep my covenant" – this was to be no compact between equals, and there was to be no bargaining. The great, victorious King was offering to take Israel as his people, but it was to be on his terms, and these had to be accepted even before they were made known. It should be noted that all that had gone before (19:4) was not being held out as a bribe. It was mentioned purely as the evidence of Jehovah's victory and of his right to demand. Israel was being left completely free to accept its deliverance from Egypt and yet refuse to be God's people.

"You shall be my own possession (*segullah*) among all peoples (*'ammim*) for all the earth is mine" – human choice almost inevitably involves rejection to a greater or less degree. If God chooses for special privilege or service, it never implies a corresponding rejection, and those not included in any particular choice may well find that it was ultimately made that they might be blessed by it and be brought by it into a wider purpose and service. Here, in announcing his choice, God specifically claims his lordship over all the earth and uses for the nations the word normally reserved for Israel (see below). The *segullah*, cf. Deut. 7:6; 14:2 and also Tit. 2:14, 1 Pet. 2:9, was that private treasure over which a king exercised sole and complete control. This is the beginning of the growing revelation that God intervenes in the life and affairs of his chosen people, be it Israel or the Church, and not only in the life of special individuals, in a way that in some measure suspends the working out of natural forces in the world around them. They need not experience what their neighbours would in a similar situation, but they cannot claim to share in their neighbours' prosperity and well-being. They are under a divine providence that baffles the wisdom of the unbeliever.

"And you shall be to me a kingdom of priests", or better, "priests over whom I rule". The common West Semitic word for priest is *komer*, but in the Old Testament it is used only for idolatrous priests, viz. 2 Ki. 23:5, Hos. 10:5, Zeph. 1:4. The common word in Hebrew is *kohen*, though seldom found outside. There is much to be said for Martin Buber's suggestion that *kohen* meant primarily an attendant on a god or king who had the right of access at any time. This would satisfactorily explain the anomalous use of the word in 2 Sam. 8:18; 20:26, and also why, in spite of the promise, priesthood in Israel was reserved to the tribe of Levi, and ideally to the house of Aaron. The priests had the responsibility of teaching the terms and requirements of the covenant and of carrying out the sacrifices and purifications that maintained it, but they did not create Israel's access to God. This may be seen especially in the Psalter, above all in psalms like 50, 51, where the necessity of sacrifice is expressly denied.

"And a holy nation (*goi*)" it is questionable whether there is much difference in practice between *goi* (nation) and *'am* (people), but as a general rule the latter is used for Israel, the former for other nations. It is therefore remarkable that in these solemn promises the usual practice should have been reversed (see above). As earlier the implication was that every people belonged to God, so here it surely is that there is no quality inherent in Israel to distinguish it from other nations except its being holy, i.e. set apart for and belonging to God. Whenever Israel wanted to be like all other nations, cf. 1 Sam. 8:5, there has been an implicit element of apostasy, though this has not necessarily been obvious.

The elders of the people accepted God's offer unconditionally without asking what he might demand (19:8), and on the third day the people were summoned to draw near the mountain by the sound of the *shophar* (19:16, 19), the ram's horn, not to be confounded with the silver trumpets of Lev. 10:1–10. This was the traditional way of announcing outstanding events to the people, whether wars (Amos 3:6, Jer. 4:5), or major religious events (Lev. 23:4; 25:9, Num. 29:1).

Sinai presented an awe-inspiring sight. Its peak was veiled in cloud, out of which came thunderclaps and flashes of lightning. As the people drew nearer to the mountain, it seemed to go up in smoke and flame, while it rocked with earthquake shocks. The immediate cause may possibly have been volcanic action, though there is no trance of it near the traditional site, but it signified the descent of the Lord.

We may reasonably ask why Mt Sinai should have taken on such a terrifying appearance. There is no difficulty in the order to fence in the mountain, for the concept of the holy, of God's separation from man, even from his own people, is basic in Old Testament thought, but that does not explain the sheer terror of the scene. Asaph was to say, "Thou didst lead thy people like a flock by the hand of Moses and Aaron" (Psa. 77:20). The people had seen God's mighty acts and terrible deeds in Egypt and at the Red Sea, but they had repeatedly, even in their murmurings, experienced his love and favour.

The answer probably lies in the dichotomy that runs throughout the Bible and can be summed up in phrases like, "It is a fearful thing to fall into the hands of the living God" (Heb. 10:31) and, "The wrath of the Lamb" (Rev. 6:16). So much of salvation history was worked out in the light of God's grace and mercy, as the shadow of the cross, which was to be, was thrown backwards, that many simply cannot give adequate weight to the wrath of God and hence propound a complete or virtually complete universalism – the opposite mistake is equally made by those who reduce the saved to a "little flock", and so exalt wrath above mercy.

Before Israel entered into a covenant with Jehovah, it had to learn the reality that Joshua was later to express, "Now therefore fear the Lord and serve him in sincerity and in faithfulness ... You cannot serve the Lord for he is a holy God" (Jos. 24:14, 15). So the terrors of the mountain served as a foil to God's opening words, "I am Jehovah your God, who brought you out of the land of Egypt, out of the house of bondage".

Any and every presentation of the Ten Words which does not start with this declaration distorts them; without it they are law, with it they are essentially the logical and inescapable sequel to God's grace. Eight of the ten are in their English translation prohibitions. But, as Martin Buber rightly pointed out, if the Hebrew is taken literally, they are a statement of what a man in true covenant relationship with God will not do, not what he should not, i.e. they say "You will not ..." As we shall see, the two positive commands, rightly understood, are open to a similar interpretation.

For many there are difficulties created by the verbal differences between Exod. 20:1–17 and Deut. 5:6–21. If we ignore the linking of the last five commandments in the latter by "and" (English "neither"), these differences are confined to the fourth and tenth. Today there is fairly general agreement that they were briefer in their original form. Moses, through whose instrumentality they were preserved, had the right both to amplify, where amplification was needed, and to vary that amplification slightly.

The first three of the Ten Words draw certain conclusions from God's redemptive acts. No power of any kind should be attributed to any other god (20:4). It is not concerned with the philosophical question of whether there can be other gods. What matters to those in covenant relationship with Jehovah is that they can be treated, if they indeed exist, as "nothingness", a term found often in Isaiah. Those who attribute undue power to demons in the Christian sphere are in danger of forgetting this.

The Ten Words were the only part of the Torah given directly by God to the whole people without an intermediary. All the rest was given through Moses (Exod. 20:19–21, cf. Gal. 3:19). In fact all that follows, whether directly in Exod. 20:22–23:23 (The Book of the Covenant), or indirectly in Lev. 18–26 (The Code of Holiness), and Deut. 12:1–30:20 (The Deuteronomic Code), is merely a commentary on the Ten Words. On their basis the covenant was sealed. All the ritual legislation, so often thought of when the Law is mentioned, was given later with the purpose of enabling mortal, weak and sinful man to remain within the covenant. Equally, when the ritual legislation found its fulfilment in the one full and perfect sacrifice, it was that man might find the principles enshrined in the Ten Words in his heart, and might by the power of the Holy Spirit carry them out in his daily walk.

The *second* (20:4–6) stresses that any attempt to depict the greatness of Jehovah, whether physically or verbally, must degrade him, and this God does not tolerate – he is "jealous". J. B. Phillips has warned us of the peril in the striking title to his book, *Your God is too Small*. Nothing reduces the attractiveness of the Gospel message more than an inadequate picture of God, which is normally linked with an inadequate life. That is why it is just here that we are given a picture of the sins of the great-grandfather working themselves out down to the great-grandson, i.e. the normal family group at the time. The low view of God and its consequences will affect all under the influence of the family head. In contrast, however, God shows steadfast love to thousands of generations of those who love him and keep his commandments. This, the traditional Jewish interpretation of "thousands", is indubitably correct, cf. p. 117.

The *third* of these commandments expresses the respect that the greatness of God should create in his people. The controversies as to the exact area covered by it are barren. It is not merely a prohibition of the irreverent or trifling use of the name of God, which should include that of Jesus. It also covers that attitude of mind which thinks that it has fully grasped God's will and ways. So often, when we say "God", or "the Holy Spirit", we really mean "I" or my understanding of God's "will". The ultra-orthodox attitude in Judaism, which first replaced Yahweh (Jehovah) by Adonai (Lord), and then Elohim (God) by various surrogates, e.g. *shem* (Name), *maqom* (Place), *shamayim* (Heaven), and now finds its bizarre expression in English by writing G-d instead of God, entirely misses the point of the commandment. Yahweh or God is being brought in, even if disguised, and it is the state of mind in which this is being done that matters.

The *fourth* word, the former of two positive ones, is really a double one; it is a command to do and to refrain from doing. The word used for labour (*'abad*) implies compulsion. In God's purpose man must work (Gen. 3:17–19, 2 Thess. 3:10). The call to remember is essentially that one should not forget that one is God's creation and hence one's life should be spent in his service; one should also see to it that one's dependants have the same possibility. Two reasons are given for the observance of the Sabbath. In

Exod. 20:11 it is that God also rested on the seventh day, but
in Gen. 2:2 this resting is explained by saying that he
desisted (*va-yishbat*) that day, cf. p. 16. The Sabbath is the
day of desisting, which implies rest, because one's work has
been finished. In Deut. 5:15 the motivation is that they were
set free from forced labour in Egypt. Therefore both they,
their family their slaves and domestic animals, as well as
their paying guests, should know freedom. The two moti-
vations are picked up in the New Testament. In Matt.
11:28–30 we have rest in spite of labour, because the labour
has become partnership with the Lord; in Heb. 4:9, 10 the
compulsion of circumstances becomes a Sabbath-keeping,
as one enters the service which is perfect freedom.

Just as the fourth word is a reminder that the freed life is in
God's world and lived for him, so the *fifth* stresses that one is
not merely a saved individual, but also a member of a saved
people. In this way it links the commandments which concern one's relationship to God with those that speak of
society. We realize our membership of society first of all in
the family, through which one was brought into being
according to God's will. But one's family owes its existence
to a wider society still. The interpretation of the commandment is not always easy, and it must be done in the
light of our Lord's words, "Render to Caesar the things that
are Caesar's, and to God the things that are God's" (Mk.
12:17). The honour that God is demanding is the recognition of his perfect wisdom in determining our sex,
our social position and our inherited talents, cf. 1 Cor.
7:17–24.

The *five commandments that follow* do not profess to introduce a list of the most heinous sins against one's fellow-men
– indeed, such a list would be contrary to scriptural principles, for it is the motive behind the act that determines the
magnitude of the evil in God's sight. They are rather those
things which are essentially a denial of one's covenant relationship to God and to one's fellow-men.

God is the only giver of life, and the taking of life is the one action where no form of reparation is really possible. Strikingly enough the first four prohibitions are really linked together by this concept, even though it is only the first of them that expressly mentions murder. There is no prohibition here of war or of judicial execution, however much this may be claimed by some. The fact of war and of the need of judicial execution are recognized in Scripture, even though they may create one of the greatest moral problems for Christians. The word used here, *ratzah*, is found only in contexts where the killing has not been authorized by due authority, i.e. it can always be rendered "to murder".

As may be seen especially in Ezek. 22 "shedding of blood", i.e. murder, can have a much wider meaning in God's sight than the mere act of killing. When we speak of adultery, we normally think of its sexual aspect, but as its use to describe idolatry shows, the Bible is really thinking of the breaking of the covenant bond of marriage, which so often destroys the family, which God had instituted as the basis of society. The modern stress on the dangers of the broken home is sufficient to show that our linking of it with murder is not fanciful.

In exactly the same way theft, especially in a society which knew neither insurance nor state welfare, and in which the majority of the population lived near the poverty line, could well bring disaster and death in its train. In addition, theft, whether underhanded and undetected, or carried out openly by the strong and mighty against whom there was no redress, was bound to break up the unity of society either by distrust or deep resentment.

The popular saying, "Give a dog a bad name and you might as well hang him", is unfortunately all too true. There is no reason for thinking that the prohibition of bearing false witness refers especially to the courts of law. Even though many an innocent person has been destroyed by false evidence, equal and perhaps greater damage can be done by whispered slander and malicious gossip, as well as by the passing on of hearsay stories which have not been checked.

There is a double evil in coveting. It is an insult to God and his love, for it suggests that his giving has been inadequate and unfair, or that he will not judge, where the things coveted have been obtained by improper means. Then it shows lack of love towards others, for it implies the willingness to see them deprived of what they have, if only one's own desires can be satisfied. Behind coveting lies lack of love, and as Hosea was later to stress, God's covenant love (*hesed*) expects a corresponding love linking the individual members of his covenant people.

When Jeremiah foretold the making of a new covenant (31:31–34) because the old had been broken, since it had come from outside, not from man's heart, he did not mention a new Torah. It was not the basis of the old covenant that was at fault; it was its inability to guarantee its being kept. The clear implication is that the basis of the old remained. Where it is understood as expounded above, a statement of the manner in which the man who has really experienced God's redemption through a new birth will live, this should obviously be the case.

Whether or not the Ten Words are recited in Christian worship, whether in full, or in our Lord's summary of them (Mk. 12:29–31), should never be allowed to become a matter of controversy among Christians. What is important is that we should never forget, nor be allowed to forget that here we have an outline of the type of life the man in true covenant relationship to God will live, though the New Testament adds some strands, which deepen it.

(The term *Torah* used frequently in this chapter, represents the biblical and rabbinic term for the Mosaic revelation as a whole. Though it is translated *law*, it really means *instruction*, and indicates that God was doing more than giving a mere series of commandments. The term *Ten Words* is the regular Jewish expression for the Ten Commandments. It is here used to indicate that we are dealing with more than commands.)

CHAPTER 12

THE CHARACTER OF GOD
(*Exod. 34*)

At the Sea of Reeds Israel had sung, "I will sing to Jehovah, for he has triumphed gloriously", and at Sinai its elders had cheerfully and sincerely said, "All that Jehovah has spoken we will do". Yet when God did speak "the people were afraid and trembled; and they stood afar off". In spite of that, or if we apply the principle of Paul's words in Rom. 1:21–23, just because of that, they picture Jehovah as a deity who would stand or sit enthroned on a golden bull,[1] and so be more comfortable to deal with. In other words, though they had experienced the grace, power and salvation of God, they did not really know him.

On a much higher plane the same was true of Moses. At the burning bush he had recognized beyond doubt that the God of his fathers was speaking to him, but he clearly doubted that God could or would accomplish his purposes through him. He returned to Egypt under God's compulsion, but twice we find him expressing doubt about God's actions (Exod. 5:22, 23; 6:30). Then, as suggested by Exod. 14:15, there was renewed doubt by the Sea of Reeds. We rightly admire his offer to die for the people after the sin of the golden bull (Exod. 32:31, 32), but, it is clear that he soon

---

[1] Cf. W. F. Albright, *From the Stone Age to Christianity*, pp. 229f. It should be clear from Exod. 32:5 that we are dealing with a debased worship of Jehovah, not with that of another god. The Hebrew *'egel*, normally translated calf, means a young bull in its full strength.

realized that it was easier to die for the people of God than to
live as their leader.

God interpreted Moses' request that he might see God's
glory (Exod. 33:18) by saying, "You cannot see my Face"
(Exod. 33:20). The Hebrew for glory (*kabod*) really means
"weight". The Semitic concept was that a man's glory is
that which gives him weight and reality, his character, his
inner man, and this is expressed above all in his face. In
other words Moses was acknowledging that he needed to
know God in a new way, if he was to accomplish the task to
which he had been called. God's statement that Moses could
see his back but not his face – in fact the sequel gives no
suggestion of such a vision – suggests that the character of
God, his glory, can be grasped only in limited measure by
man. The fullest revelation that can be granted to man is
"the light of the knowledge of the glory of God in the face of
Christ" (2 Cor. 4:6). The mystic's dream that he can pene-
trate further has no basis in Scripture.

The validity of this interpretation is supported by the
revelation's being apparently entirely a verbal one (Exod.
33:19; 34:5, 6), though we must not minimize the awe-
fulness of the theophany. But though Moses prostrated
himself in awe, there is no suggestion of his being overwhelmed as in the case of some other theophanies.

The Old Testament is not given to quoting previous
revelations, except indirectly, but the bulk of this passage is
met with five times elsewhere as well as a number of
reminiscences of it. It is worth noting also that this passage
plays a major part in the Synagogue services as well.

The revelation began with a two-fold repetition of the
name Jehovah (*Yahweh, Yahweh*), the name that had already
been pronounced at the bush and explained by the formula,
"I will be that I will be" (Exod. 3:14). Nothing that would
follow or would be revealed would deny that which was
past, and nothing in the future would exhaust God's revelation of himself until his glory was seen in the face of Jesus
Christ. It is the failure to grasp this principle that makes

many Christians feel that the Old Testament has little or no meaning for them; they even suggest that they have in measure outgrown the New Testament revelation of the Christ.

The revelation went on: "A God merciful and gracious" (*'el raḥum ve-ḥanun*). The use here of El rather than Elohim may simply suggest that we have an ancient liturgical formula, but it is more likely that we should look back to the basic meaning – A Strong One who is merciful and gracious, unlike the strength of earth's great ones, which is used above all to oppress. But there is more than that here; *raḥum* is from the same root as *reḥem*, the mother's womb. God is not merely the great Creator, but he loves all that he has made with a deep understanding of its weakness and need. "Compassionate" (NEB, TEV) is probably a preferable rendering, though we might consider "tenderness" (JB). In addition, this compassionate love is not a response to any merits of his creation, but simply to their need. Though, immediately after, God stressed the reality of his wrath, he placed his love in the first place. Any presentation of the Gospel which reverses this order distorts it.

"Slow to anger but plenteous in covenant love (*ḥesed*) and faithfulness (*'emet*)". Scripture makes it abundantly clear what the things are that awaken God's anger. In general terms it is the suppression of truth (Rom. 1:18). This finds its supreme evil in causing "one of these little ones who believe in me to stumble" (Mk. 9:42); in other words the deliberate effort to destroy that which is good. "Slow to anger": man is swift to judge and indeed to punish, where he possesses the power. With God, however, it would seem that he holds his hand until it becomes completely clear that there is no hope of reformation. In the Old Testament this is made plain in connection both with the Northern Kingdom (2 Kings 17:7–18) and with Judah (2 Kings 21:10–15; 23:26, 27). In the New this is one of the dominating concepts of *Revelation.*

"Plenteous in covenant love and faithfulness": the force

of "plenteous" is probably not the extent of God's love and faithfulness, but that they far exceed anything that man expects. It is not likely that covenant love is here referring exclusively to the Sinaitic covenant or even only to formal covenants like those with Noah and Abraham, though the thought of Sinai will be uppermost. Down the ages men and women in the hour of their despair have turned from the deities created by man's imaginings to an unknown power above and beyond them and have been heard. This is what the Puritans called the uncovenanted mercies of God. Where, however, men have come in measure to know God, have trusted and obeyed him, they have always found him more loving and faithful than they had expected. The climax, of course, comes to the Christian, who having come to know God's glory in Jesus Christ, can say, "He who did not spare his own Son but gave him up for us all, will he not also give us all things with him?" (Rom. 8:32).

"Keeping covenant love for thousands (of generations)": this, the rabbinic interpretation, is based on the contrast in Exod. 20:5, 6, cf. p. 110. While punishment may pass on to the fourth generation, there is no such limitation on God's love and faithfulness. It is impossible for us to realize the extent of the blessings we enjoy because of our ancestors' faith. This is not a question of the merits of the fathers that play a great role in rabbinic thinking but of God's faithfulness.

"Bearing crookedness and rebellion and sin": the normal rendering, viz. "forgiving", is technically correct, but it seems to miss the main implication. There are two main terms used in Hebrew with the sense of to forgive or pardon, *salaḥ* and *nasa'*. The former seems to be an exact equivalent of the English and implies the remitting of whatever penalty may be due. The latter, however, means to lift up, to carry; when it is used with the sense of "forgive", it seems to mean more than just the lifting of the penalty but stresses something the modern man is all too willing to forget, viz. forgiveness can very well imply that the one

who forgives must sometimes pay a penalty himself. A boy
playing in the garden with his ball may accidentally break
the neighbour's window. Just because his father forgives
him, i.e. he does not dock his pocket-money to pay for a
new pane of glass, he will have to pay for the damage
himself. In other words forgiveness very often involves
bearing the consequences.

In most cases it is impossible to decide why one or other
of these words is used, but in a key passage like this it cannot
be accidental that we find the latter. It is true that while *nasa'*
is sometimes used of human forgiveness, *salah* is applied
only to God's. Since, however, the total number of cases
where it is a question of human forgiveness is very small,
this could be the result of accident; argument from silence
alone is always dangerous. Centuries were to elapse before
Isaiah was given the vision of the Servant of Jehovah
bearing our griefs and carrying our sorrows, on whom was
the chastisement that makes us whole (Isa. 53:5). We can
hardly affirm that Moses realized the full implication
of God's words, but equally he cannot have missed their
essential implications.

The broken-hearted sinner may say with David,
"Against thee, thee only, have I sinned, and done that
which is evil in thy sight", but neither in his nor in David's
case is it true, except in the sense that behind all the wrong
and suffering caused to others lies the sin against God.
Those who speak so lightly of God's forgiveness are insofar
correct that there are no obstacles preventing God's forgiveness of the wrongs done exclusively to him, if indeed
such exist, but he has no right to forgive the wrongs done to
others and their effects, far more far-reaching than most
even begin to realize. To do that he must bear their consequences, so "God was in Christ reconciling the world to
himself" (2 Cor. 5:19). This helps to explain Jesus' insis-
tence on the relationship of forgiving and being forgiven. I
have no right to refuse forgiveness, for my Lord has borne
the results of the other's sin against me.

Man's sin is summed up in three words, though others are to be found elsewhere: *'avon, pesha', hatta'ah*. "Iniquity" is overwhelmingly the rendering in the English versions for *'avon*, though this does not apply to JB, which uses a variety of translations, few of which seem to be adequate, especially here, where it gives "faults". Our understanding has been made more difficult by the frequent use in AV, followed in part by RSV, of "iniquity" for *'aven*, an entirely different word. In spite of the venerable tradition behind it we must reject it. Few who use the word "iniquity" realize that it means "injustice", which is in fact the meaning of *'aven*; *'avon* seems to stress man's crookedness, the acts that come from it and the guilt it brings. David regarded it as part of human heritage; "Behold I was brought forth in *'avon*" (Psa. 51:5). This was expressed less forcibly by Job. "Who can bring a clean thing out of an unclean?" (14:4), cf. 15:14; 25:4. For reasons outside the scope of this study the tendency of the New Testament is to include the three aspects of man's falling short of the glory of God under the term sin. Hence we can easily fail to grasp that in his description of indwelling sin in Rom. 7 Paul is describing the results of man's inborn crookedness, which the rabbis named less forcibly the *yetzer ra'*, the evil impulse or principle in man, only partially counterbalanced by the *yetzer tob*, the good impulse or principle.

For *pesha'* we find in the AV "transgression" eighty-four times in contrast to three other renderings, occurring together only nine times. This is an adequate rendering for those who think of its meaning, but "rebellion" seems better, for the word does not imply the accidental but only the deliberate infringement of the guide lines and regulations laid down by lawful authority, be it God's or that of an earthly ruler. Man's longing for freedom varies with his upbringing. There are societies in which the young are brain-washed at an early stage into accepting the traditional existing standards of authority; there are others where the severity of the penalties for the rebel have the same effect. In both these types of society the religious sanctions are at least as strong as the social ones. In contrast, other forms of society extol the ideal of freedom, though in practice even the anarchist finds himself forced to set some limits which may not be passed. Whatever type of society a person finds himself in, history shows his willingness to revolt against its rules, whether they claim to be human or religious, or whether, as in orthodox Judaism, the two have amalgamated.

Periodically, we find that some catastrophe has been caused by someone's failure to follow the rules, on the road or rail, on the seas, in mines or factories. It matters little whether the failure was due to carelessness or was deliberate; the damage done was inevitable and irremediable. But for every case where the disastrous results of rebellion or carelessness become known, there must be hundreds and thousands which will be revealed only on the day of judgment. In very deed, unless God bears it, we are lost, if justice sits enthroned.

It should be noted that Scripture nowhere suggests that God uses his almighty power to counter the principles he has built into his creation and so save men from the results of their actions. It is clear that he may do so in the face of ignorance and accident, but it is doubtful whether he ever does so, where man has deliberately flouted his will. When God's Man bore our sins on the cross, there was no attempt to minimize the burden that had to be borne by him.

hatta'ah, found only twice, is apparently only an extended form of *hatt'at*. The basic meaning behind *hatt'at* and *het'* is "missing the mark". There seems to be no difference at all between these two forms, except that the former is used 135 times for the sin offering as against 155 times with the force of "sin", its guilt or its punishment. The shorter form is found only 34 times, but never for the sin offering. Both words are rarely used of our failings towards men, but in every case where they are, they are those who have a claim on our obedience. In other words the standard or mark we fail to reach is one fixed by due authority, divine or human. This shows that John Wesley was mistaken when he suggested that sin involved only positive action, for the failure could and often does come from inaction. It rules out, however, the suggestion that failure to conform to normal human expectations need necessarily be sinful, and Paul makes it clear that we cannot speak of sin, where the standard is unknown or has not been given (Rom. 5:13).

Though God bears and forgives, yet he "will by no means clear the guilty", i.e. he will not leave him unpunished, cf. Exod. 20:7. The probable meaning is that given by rabbinic tradition, viz. pardon for the penitent, punishment of the impenitent. At the same time the interpretation hardly does justice to the force of the Hebrew. Forgiveness or punishment, yes, but crookedness, rebellion and sin are not removed by either, something that is all too often forgotten. We are facing the mystery of the cross, which could not be made clear until the eternal purpose of God was made a reality in time.

NEB links the clause closely with the following, as does TEV much more freely, and renders "and not sweeping the guilty clean away; but one who punishes sons and grandsons ..." This in itself is an attractive rendering, but it is questionable whether the Hebrew will really bear the meaning. It is also rendered the more doubtful, because it ignores the obvious parallel with Exod. 20:7. Knox is, as so often, very free, but there is much to be said for his rendering, "None can claim innocence in his own right". Ultimately the man that stands in judgment will not be able to appeal to ignorance, to the example of others, or to virtually intolerable circumstances. In the last analysis man's only hope is in the atonement wrought by God himself, however man's finite mind may seek to explain it. Fortunately it is not our understanding of it that makes it effective.

There is no need to deal here with the coming of judgment on the children and children's children to the third and fourth generation, for it was explained in the last chapter in connection with the Fourth Commandment, cf. p. 109 f. Here it is sufficient to stress that because no one lives to himself and no one dies to himself, our failure and rebellion cannot be confined in their results to ourselves, yet God is so merciful, that even here a limitation is placed on the evil we have wrought.

There was only one possible response to this revelation: "Moses made haste, bowed to the ground and prostrated himself" (NEB) – the usual rendering, "worshipped", is misleading for the modern reader. He acknowledged the people's crookedness and failure. He did not mention the rebellion of the golden bull. That had been forgiven, and there was no necessary reason why it, or something similar should be repeated, but the inbred crookedness made certain that failure would continue. In spite of that, but just because of the character of Jehovah, which had just been revealed, he prayed God the King *(Adonai)* to go in the midst of them and take them as his *naḥalah* (inheritance or possession). The traditional English versions prefer the former rendering, but it carries the wrong connotation for the modern reader. That which one had acquired by inheritance was in the thought of the time inalienable in a way that what one obtained for oneself by skill and hard work was not. So, in a context like this, the word bears the sense of inalienable possession, a thought which elsewhere is expressed by Israel's being called Jehovah's first-born or wife. Nothing will ultimately separate Jehovah from his people.

INDEXES

NAMES AND SUBJECTS
Items sufficiently indicated by chapter headings not included

HEBREW WORDS QUOTED

SCRIPTURAL REFERENCES

Those sufficiently indicated by chapter headings are not included

P. 14

— 800 generations the Bible has brought
to men the essential spiritual fact
behind God's creating.

P. 15